REMOVE THE HEART OF STONE

Remove the Heart of Stone

Charismatic Renewal and the Experience of Grace

DONAL DORR

'I shall give you a new heart, and put a new spirit
in you; I shall remove the heart of stone from your
bodies and give you a heart of flesh instead.'

Ezekiel 36 : 26

PAULIST PRESS
New York/Ramsey/Toronto

289. 9

D737

8009011

ISBN: 0-8091-2119-0

Published by Paulist Press
Editorial Office: 1865 Broadway, N.Y., N.Y. 10023
Business Office: 545 Island Road, Ramsey, N.J. 07446
Printed in England

CONTENTS

INTRODUCTION

This is a time of convergence. We've had a decade of exploration of human experience in its personal, interpersonal, and public aspects. Now one has the sense that many of these paths are converging, that they open out on to the same clearing. It is a good time to pause and exchange experiences before we plunge forward again.

This book is an invitation to pause in this way. It is addressed to the many people who sense the convergence of different aspects of their experience. It is also addressed to the many others who have been so single-minded that they have had no time to have such a sense of convergence. These are the explorers, who are so enthralled by one path that they see it as the only correct one. Some choose the path of transcendental meditation or of yoga; others choose liberation theology, or transactional analysis, or the thirty-days retreat, or charismatic renewal. In a world where so many find themselves quite lost, it is good that these people have found some path. But how much better if they could look around and relate their experience to that of others.

One great convergence of our time is that between the different Christian traditions. The theological and institutional levels of the ecumenical movement are obvious. There is, however, a less obvious but more significant convergence: many good Christians now find that they respond to elements in the spirituality of other strands of Christianity. This convergence in spirituality can be seen as an impulse of the Spirit, coming to bring new life and hope at a time when the ecumenical movement seemed to some to be flagging. It brings Christians together at a level deeper than theology or institutions. More and more people feel called to share together in prayer, in spite of their denominational differences. This movement for shared prayer is associated especially with the Charismatic Renewal.

The most surprising thing about the Charismatic Renewal is that its immediate roots are neither Protestant nor Catholic, Anglican nor Orthodox. It is rooted in Pentecostalism,[1] a strand of Christianity which had scarcely been involved at all in the ecumenical movement. I recall hearing Professor Francis O'Sullivan of the Gregorian University speak very movingly on this topic at a prayer-meeting in Rome during Christian Unity Week in 1976. Noting that God chooses the despised and the weak to confound the strong, he pointed out that God had given a special role to the Pentecostalists whom we in the historic Churches had rather looked down on: they were chosen to teach us again how to praise God—and to bring us together in doing so. One might add that they have also taught us much about spontaneous prayer, about prayer for healing, and about openness to the gifts of the Spirit. And as we learn from them, they are coming to accept that we too may have a genuine Christian experience and that they may have something to learn from us.

My main purpose in this book is to recognise and promote the convergence between Christian traditions and spiritualities that has been brought about by the Charismatic Renewal. There are many points at which this convergence is taking place. But I shall focus attention chiefly on one—the one I believe to be of central importance. This is the experience which those in the Pentecostal tradition generally call 'baptism in the Spirit'. I shall try to show that a great enrichment of Christianity can come from taking very seriously the basic insights and emphases of the Pentecostal, the Catholic and the Protestant traditions as they relate to this question. For instance:

—The Protestant tradition rightly emphasises the centrality of salvation by grace through faith.
—The Pentecostal tradition is quite right to insist that the real Christian should be aware of being filled with the Spirit and led by the Spirit.
—And the Catholic tradition has a great deal to contribute from its sacramental theology, its mystical tradition, and its emphasis on the basic harmony between the natural order and the order of grace.[2]

The term 'baptism in the Spirit', though scriptural in its origins, has been appropriated by those in the Pentecostal tradition. A good deal of clarification of what it means, or should mean, is required before the term can be fully at home in the Protestant and Catholic traditions. Most of this book is concerned with providing such a clarification. But agreement on the use of *language* is not really the central issue. My principal concern is for the mutual enrichment that can come from agreement (or even greater convergence) on the *reality* behind the language. I believe that the passage from Ezekiel quoted on the title-page of the book indicates this reality in a way that transcends the variation in language between the different traditions: 'I shall give you a new heart . . . I shall remove the heart of stone . . . and give you a heart of flesh.'

That 'new heart' is the source of Christian experience. And this is a book about Christian experience. Not that it covers every aspect of it. For instance, there are political aspects which are scarcely touched on here. Although I consider them basic to what it means to be a Christian, I shall resist the temptation to drag them in. For the topic here is a more personal aspect of liberation. However, it must be noted that personal and political liberation have for too long been opposed as if one had to choose to go in one of two different directions. Now at last there is a convergence of the two.[3] The personal liberation which is our topic here must accompany and underpin the Christian's commitment to liberation in the public sphere.

In this book we shall focus attention on the process by which the Christian first comes to experience the full effects of faith. This involves a major breakthrough, a transformation of the person's world. But does it have to take place suddenly; could it not equally well take place in a gradual and cumulative way? And in what sense can one be a Christian at all without such a breakthrough? And what can be done to facilitate its occurrence? These are some of the questions we shall try to answer in the course of the book.

In trying to answer them we shall take account of another very significant convergence of our time—that between developments in the understanding of religion and developments in the human sciences of psychology and sociology. The more we understand of the psychology of personal development and the psychology and sociology of groups, the better we can understand and co-operate with the action of God's grace. In the final chapters of the book I shall consider the specifically religious problem of how to 'let go' to God. In doing so I shall try to make use of some of the insights of psychology and sociology.

The book is ultimately pastoral and practical in its purpose. Not in the sense of providing a set of instructions for making faith come alive. Faith is a gift, not to be manipulated in this way. What can be attempted is rather more modest: to help people to co-ordinate different elements in their own experience and that of their friends. This could bring about a better understanding of what it means to 'let go' to God and to others; it could even facilitate the process.

If people are to be helped in this way it will be not just by the contents of the book but perhaps more particularly by its style. It must convey a sense of pausing where the paths converge, pausing to reflect and share experiences. I would like it to evoke a mood that is both religious and reflective. To explain what I mean, let me recall Wordsworth's definition of poetry as 'emotion recollected in tranquillity', and consider these words one by one:

—'Emotion': What is required is something less abstract, less removed from the real stuff of life, than the older style of theological writing. Something that will resonate with the reader's own experience. Of course this must not be just raw emotion. Rather it is a total human experience, including emotion.[4] Feelings are particularly important when we are dealing with religious realities. For in religion, as in art, it is hard to pin down responses and values in exact rational concepts. Often we have to depend on feelings to give hints and intimations of what is involved. Not of course that we ought always be led by our immediate feelings. Rather we must try to distinguish between various kinds of feelings and the various directions in which they can lead. This process of discernment is a major part of the challenge of living out our faith.

—'Recollected': What is in question is not the immediate experience but a reflection on it, an articulation and interpretation of it. Normally this reflection will be rooted in the writer's own experience. But it cannot end there. It must relate this experience to that of others. This begins with the local Christian community and extends outwards in ever widening circles of space and time to the whole Christian community. Then it goes beyond that again to take account of religious experience in the wider community of the human race.

—'In tranquillity': It is important that there be a certain pause between the experience and the articulation of it. Such a cooling off period can help to bring objectivity and depth into one's reflection. We find today a lot of spiritual writing of the testimony type. Many people are helped by it. But others find it too obtrusively personal. Even where it is found helpful it is not a substitute for theology. Testimony can be so subjective that it lacks balance. A certain tranquillity and distancing is required if one is to articulate and interpret the Christian experience accurately and fruitfully. In this book I shall try to stay close to the living experience of Christian faith. But I hope also to provide a sound basis in the Bible, in tradition, in theology and in the human sciences for what I shall say. I hope, then, that it will be an instance of 'emotion recollected in tranquillity'.

Having noted the importance of experience in what I am writing I must now acknowledge the contribution of many people who shared in various ways in the experience out of which the book is written. Over the past three years the material has been emerging and being refined as I shared in, and reflected on, the experience of missionaries and the people among whom they work. It began in Nigeria, not only chronologically but in a deeper spiritual sense. Since then I've been privileged to meet, at a deep level, missionaries and local religious leaders in East and Central Africa, in the Caribbean country of Grenada, in Brazil, the USA, Rome and at home in Ireland. I am thankful to them for their generosity in sharing their experience of the faith. I am also grateful to Father Martin Tierney and the late Canon J. G. McGarry for advice and encouragement.

Donal Dorr,
Kiltegan, Ireland.
October 1977.

PART ONE

BACKGROUND—CAN WE EXPERIENCE GRACE?

1. MEETING THE GIVER IN THE GIFTS

The 1960s were the years of renewal in theology while the 1970s are years of renewal in religion. Of course this is an over-simplification. But I think it expresses a profound truth about the way the Spirit has been working in the Church.

The renewal in religion has many facets. There is a great interest in the study of religion and religions. The great world religions are interacting and learning from each other perhaps more than ever before. But at the heart of the renewal in religion is something far more personal and experimental than this. There is an astonishing growth of interest in personal religious experience. Many people from a very secular background are experimenting with religious or quasi-religious techniques. And committed Christians are concentrating far more attention than has been the custom in the past decade on the specifically religious aspects of the faith.

Over the past hundred years religion has come under very severe attack from political scientists, psychologists, sociologists, philosophers and, not least, theologians. It was dismissed as an attempt to escape from harsh political and social realities. It was accused of being a facile way of papering over the gaps in human knowledge left by an inadequate scientific understanding of the world. It was condemned as a futile attempt to make contact with God who in fact, so the theory claimed, is quite beyond the reach of any merely human effort. There was an element of truth in all these accusations. And this many-sided attack on religion has had a good result in the emergence of a purified and far more defensible conception of religion. In the past few years the scholars are coming to acknowledge the validity of the religious approach to reality, alongside such other approaches as those of the scientist or the artist.[1] One of the most distinctive features of the new approach to religion is the emphasis it puts on religious feelings.

In recent decades Christians have been rather chary of religious feelings. There were many reasons for this attitude. First of all we lived in what was called 'the age of science'—and it was the kind of science that did not do justice to feelings. Then Western Christians seem to have been very influenced by puritanism. It was considered a little disreputable to be guided by feelings—even in minor matters like choice of food, not to mention the more important areas of life like work or relationships with others. Of course most people were too sensible to base their lives entirely on such a puritan approach. But there was one area where distrust of feelings was so widespread that it was scarcely noticed. That was the area of the spiritual life—that is, the area of our explicit relationship with God.

Catholics and Protestants each had their own particular reasons for being suspicious of religious feelings. Protestants were scared of what they called 'enthusiasm'—that is, the waves of religious emotionalism which had accompanied the great Protestant revivals and had at times led to scenes of mass hysteria. Catholics had a more theological reason for distrusting feelings in the religious sphere. Catholic doctrine insisted strongly that grace is *supernatural*. This was commonly taken to mean that it belonged to a realm that is beyond ordinary human experience. So it would not be generally acceptable to speak of 'experiencing grace'—except perhaps in the case of some mystical experience, which would have been considered a rare occurrence. (In the next chapter I shall return to this basic question of the supernatural character of grace.)

Experience of grace?

In the past few years Christians have begun to speak freely of the experience of grace. At the popular level a major factor in bringing about this change has been the influence of Pentecostalism. As the Charismatic Renewal swept through the main-line Protestant Churches and the Catholic Church, many Christians in these Churches found themselves having the same kind of experiences as were recounted so vividly by members of the

Pentecostal Churches and Assemblies. They failed to find in the mainline Churches a language which seemed adequate to express these experiences. So, by and large, they simply adopted the idiom of the Pentecostalists—with some minor adjustments.

More or less parallel to this change at the popular level, there has been a change at the theological level. It has resulted in a new theological approach to grace, an approach which justifies the use of the phrase 'experience of grace'. Unfortunately this theology did not develop, or at least it did not become popularised, early enough to be of any great help to those who had to borrow the idiom of Pentecostalism to give an account of their spiritual experiences. Now, however, it is possible to hope for a fruitful dialogue between the Pentecostalist spirituality and a spirituality articulated in terms of this new theology of grace.

The new theology of grace has emerged as part of a rethink of the basic framework of our understanding of the faith. It fits in with a new theology of revelation, of faith, of history, and especially of the relationship between God and the world. It finds its deep roots in the personalist and existentialist understanding of what it means to be human. Particularly important for it is the modern insistence that to be human is to be *conscious*. Not that so elementary a point was previously ignored; but there had been a tendency to define grace in a way that did not seem to take full account of conscious human experience.

The giver in the gifts

Postponing to the next chapter a more detailed theological account of the relationship between the new and the old theologies of grace, I would like here to give a general account of what I mean by the experience of grace. It involves using the word 'grace' in a way that is rather different to that in which I would have used it some years ago. But I believe that the change does not involve a radical break with the past. Rather it involves focusing on aspects that were more or less implicit previously. Fundamentally it involves giving priority in the account of grace to one's relationship with God, rather than to some intrinsic change in the constitution of the person.

'Grace' now means for me any or all of the gifts of God, in so far as I recognise the Giver in the gifts. Alternatively, I could say, 'grace' means God making himself personally present to me in a variety of different ways:

—in the events of my daily life, where I recognise his fatherly providence;

—in the pattern of human history, where I believe he is involved and is revealing his concern for us;

—in my personal conviction that I myself and the world are liberated by Christ, and therefore not totally at the mercy of the evil which I experience as very real and threatening both within my own being and in the world around me;

—in the sense of being accepted and 'affirmed' in spite of my weakness and my guilt—even in a way that transforms my faults into an occasion for a deeper healing love;

—in the desire to pray—some tiny spark of which I discover within me even in times of dissipation, desolation or dryness;

—in the patience and tenderness of my friends in whom I can see the gifts of God poured out so lavishly that they are eager to share these gifts, and themselves, with me;

—in the hope which I can at times share with those who are sick, depressed or troubled;

—above all in the primal gift of faith which underpins all these graces and unfolds itself by taking concrete expression in them.

It is clear that in this approach grace is a universal reality. But this is not the kind of universality that means nothing because it embraces everything. Materially, grace is or can be everything in me and around me. Formally, however, it is any or all of these experienced as a personal gift from God, a revelation of his love, a means of dialogue with him. So, paradoxically, grace in its strictest sense is not of this world at all. Rather it is the link between our world and the Transcendent Other.

Gift of faith

I now think of faith in its basic sense as the key that opens up for me the world of grace. More concretely we can describe faith as 'the ability to see God in all things'. Obviously we cannot take the word 'see' in its literal sense. So, to clarify what is meant we can add that faith is the ability to interpret reality as the gift of God. The word 'interpret' could also be misleading, for it suggests a deliberate activity. Whereas faith is prior to such deliberation—though it will normally continue into our deliberate thinking and choosing. Faith is that within me which, against all expectation, enables me to experience the nearness and concern of God, by recognising him in the pattern of my life. It convinces me that the world is enfolded in God's love and is moving towards fulfilment in him.

The first moment, then, of faith is the recognition of God. This leads to a second moment which is my free response to his presence. It includes elements of acceptance, joy, thanks and praise. This response is itself experienced as having the character of gift. So gift permeates every aspect of faith, including the point where it is a free response to the presence of God.

This gift of faith is not an all-or-nothing affair. There are many degrees and kinds of faith. There are variations in the comprehensiveness of faith; in principle it should permeate every part of one's consciousness but in fact it may be operative only in some areas. Psychological and cultural blocks may inhibit the religious experience or limit the extent to which it permeates consciousness or the manner in which it interacts with other modes of consciousness. Faith can also vary in explicitness, from a vague sense of being touched by the Transcendent to a highly developed awareness of being cared for and drawn by the Father, saved and 'incorporated' by Jesus Christ, led and prayed in by the Spirit. Variations in the intensity of faith also occur: it may be present so strongly that the person is scarcely aware of anything else but the presence of God; at other times it may recede so as to become just part of the background awareness against which everyday feelings, thoughts and decisions take place. Faith varies also in the *mood* it evokes—a sense of acceptance may be dominant at one time, at another time a sense of being shattered, or even of being abandoned ('Why have you forsaken me?'—*Matt.* 27: 46). In addition to all these variations, faith is capable of growth; and there is therefore the possibility of unbalanced or misdirected growth and the aberrations resulting from this.

Problem of language

The experience of grace is the personal discovery of a link between our world and a transcendent beyond. The character of that link cannot be adequately described by our human language since our words and meanings apply properly to the realities and relationships of this world. But we can use the traditional *via negativa* (the negative way) and *via eminentiae* (the way of going further) to point in the direction along which grace lies. We can say that the link between the worlds is not less than an inter-personal one. Not that such personal words as 'dialogue' and 'love' have precisely the same connotation when applied to our relations with God as to our relations with each other. But it is far more accurate to maintain that we can love and be loved by the 'terrible Other' than to say that love does not describe the relationship. Similarly we are entitled, even compelled, to make use of the words 'speak' and 'listen' when referring to our rela-tionship with the Incomprehensible, the Silent One. We can even 'argue' with the Whirlwind until he chooses to silence us (*Job* 38 and 40). Our Judaeo-Christian tradition encourages us to make the fullest use of such interpersonal words; and, for the Chris-tian, faith in Jesus Christ involves the conviction that God has quite literally spoken and heard human words, that God loves and is loved as a human. Nevertheless such interpersonal language has to be supplemented, even corrected. This becomes possible by making use of mystical language. At this point the mystical current in our tradition finds much common ground with the mysticism of other great religious traditions—of Hinduism, Buddhism and Islam.

What is the best term to apply to the way contact is estab-lished between the human consciousness and the Transcendent? Obviously we do not *feel* God in any purely physical sense. Nor do we *see* or *hear* God as such. Neither is our contact primarily through conceptual knowledge; or at least our conceptual know-ledge must be underpinned by a more primordial experiential contact. Nor is our contact purely a matter of blind volition—a loyal acceptance and acting 'as if' we could hear or feel God; though there are certain dark nights of faith when this is very nearly the case. Some philosophers and theologians postulate in us a distinct faculty through which we come in contact with God. But this seems to isolate the religious experience unduly. It seems better to think in terms of a religious *mood* or *mode* of consciousness. For the person in this mood or mode, an awareness of God permeates every level of consciousness.

Spiritual feelings

The term 'spiritual feelings' seems to be the most appropriate one to designate what is involved. The word 'feeling' conveys the spontaneous quality of the religious awareness; there is a givenness which is prior to any rational analysis or decision. The word 'spiritual' distinguishes these feelings from more commonplace, empirical feelings. Not that one can specify an exact boundary between the two kinds of feelings. For the human person is a spirit and a certain spiritual quality pervades all acts of consciousness. Religious feelings cannot be sharply distinguished from secular feelings in terms of their content or object. The difference is one of context and mood. For instance the feeling of serenity or the feeling of loneliness may be experienced in a non-religious mood. But they may also be intensely religious feelings in which I experience the presence or the presence-in-absence of God.

What then are we to say in practice about the feelings of deep joy, peace, and hope which are often experienced in personal or group prayer? Are they 'merely human' feelings which might at most be effects or occasions of God's grace? Or are they themselves the gifts and graces of the Spirit as many Pentecostalists and 'charismatics' would maintain? I think each of these views is partly right and partly wrong. Such feelings are truly human. But they are truly grace and gifts of God in so far as we experience the presence of God in and through them. They are no longer 'merely human' because they are now in a different context. It is not just that some religious overtones are added on to them from outside. Part of the actual experience itself is the sense that these feelings are the free gifts of God, the sense that in this experience God is touching the heart.

So we are entitled to speak of these feelings of joy, peace and hope as graces or as gifts of the Spirit, provided we are considering them in their context. But it would be a mistake to consider the feelings as such to be graces in any privileged sense—for instance as indisputable proofs of God's presence. It is only when they are 'read' in the light of faith that they present themselves as coming from the hand of God. They do not then dispense one from the need to have faith. But when experienced by the believer they undoubtedly build up his or her faith.

Prayer

Our awareness of God's presence is nourished by prayer. Not just the spontaneous prayer that can well up in us at any time. But the prayer that is time out from immediate concerns, the prayer that requires hours given, and effort spent, and dryness endured. When we reach out in this way our efforts may lead to a vivid sense of God's presence. But God refuses to establish an exact proportion between our efforts at any given time and the attainment of an experienced contact with him.

Sometimes our awareness of God's presence just 'happens' spontaneously. It is experienced as more gratuitous than usual, less mediated by, or less dependent on, our attempts to reach him. An experience of this kind can bring home to us that God cannot be grasped by any human effort. I cannot reach out and 'touch' God at a time of my own choosing. Rather I must wait on him and allow him to touch me when and how he chooses.

Generally speaking, it is not very helpful to make a distinction between a direct and an indirect experience of God's presence, since the words 'direct' and 'indirect' apply more properly to relationships with things or people in this world rather than to our contact with the Transcendent. However, anybody who reads the mystics must recognise a qualitative difference between what they speak of and the 'ordinary' experience of grace. This difference in quality could justify a metaphorical or analogous use of the phrase 'direct experience of God' to describe the mystical sense of union with God.

Suffering and dryness

Some Church leaders have become rather worried in recent years because they find so much stress being put on spiritual *feelings*. They fear that Christians who must endure trials or dryness may think they are untouched by the grace of God and are lacking in real faith. There is some justification for these worries. Some individuals may have been misled in this way. Perhaps it is inevitable that the new way of thinking about grace should at times be misunderstood—particularly since the Pentecostal tradition, which is one of its sources, itself suffers from confusion on this point.

One of the main aims of this book is to clarify the issue and eliminate such misunderstandings. Already at this stage it is well to insist that there is no question of identifying grace with a happy feeling. The Christian, as we shall see, may be led through the dark valley (*Ps.* 23:4). If Christ himself had to suffer spiritual anguish in his agony and a sense of dereliction on the cross, how could his followers expect to be immune from trial? A sense of absence of God, of deep spiritual dryness, is itself an important spiritual feeling which can play an important role in the life of the Christian.[2]

The roots of religion

Experiences of grace are the roots from which the whole of organised religion draws life. Any effective talking about God or religion presupposes that the person to whom one is speaking has had similar experiences; otherwise the exercise is as pointless as trying to convey to someone born blind what it means to see.

There are practical applications arising from this. Preaching or teaching about God or about anything in the religious world is not to be seen primarily as communicating knowledge or forming attitudes. It is first of all a matter of helping people to locate and advert to the religious experiences they have themselves. This leads on to a fostering of such experiences. Then one can help them to interpret such experiences and to work out their implications, by relating them to the experience, words, and behaviour of others. In this process the Christian gives a normative role to Christ and the Christian community; but increasingly we must also take account of the way religious experience is handled in other religious traditions.

The theological renewal of the sixties broke down the thought-system which prevented us seeing the importance or even the possibility of experiencing grace. The more important renewal now taking place results in a new spirituality rather than just a new theology. This is not just a new spirituality in the sense of a different theory about the 'spiritual life', but a change in outlook, a different approach, a sensitivity to something quite different to what we considered important in the past. We are learning to pay heed to our spiritual feelings.

New world?

It is an exciting world that is opened up for us by this new spirituality. A world where God is experienced as real, alive, relevant and, above all, near and concerned. A world swept by spiritual forces to which we become attuned by adverting to the spiritual currents flowing through our consciousness. A world of people, to whom we become opened up by becoming sensitive to their feelings and therefore less self-centred and more vulnerable.

It is a dangerous world too. For our spiritual feelings are not unambiguously good and trustworthy. Coming from a heart which may not be fully converted, they can be muddled or distorted. So we have to learn techniques of discernment, ways of distinguishing between different kinds of feeling in order to interpret them and to know when and how to be guided by them.

The challenge of discernment which faces each of us is well summed up in the following passage by George Aschenbrenner,

> . . . welling up in the consciousness and experience of each of us are two spontaneities, one good and for God, another evil and not for God. . . . For one eager to love God with his or her whole being, the challenge is not simply to let the spontaneous happen but rather to be able to sift out these various spontaneous urges and give full existential ratification to those spontaneous feelings that are from and for God.[3]

Revolution or growth?

The renewal that is taking place can be experienced and interpreted either in terms of a model of growth and continuity or in

terms of a model of revolution. I have just described it as opening
up a new world. This suggests that I am thinking of it as a
revolutionary break with the past. It is true that for many
people there is the sense of a startlingly sharp break with
an approach to spirituality that was very rationalistic and legalistic. In this sense there may be a kind of personal revolution
involved. But in other ways there is very real continuity with
the past.

The situation is rather similar to that which existed during the
dramatic theological developments of the 1960s. Those who were
actively involved in constructing the new theological climate
could experience their work as building on the past in many ways;
indeed it was frequently a return to a more fundamental past
than the immediate past. But many who looked at the new trends
from the outside felt that there was a revolution going on, a
radical rejection of the past. And this assessment was shared by
some of the more superficial proponents of the new theology. In
much the same way we can find today elements of continuity and
elements of discontinuity in the new approach to religious
experience. The former are more evident to those who are actively
involved in creating the new spirituality. They are conscious of
building on the past. Indeed, much of what might appear to be a
break with the traditional approach is for them a return to an
older and more authentic tradition.

The experience of grace and the process of discernment of
which we are speaking are as old as Christianity—and indeed as
old as any genuine religion. They are prominent in the life of
Christ and the early Church. Saints in every age have written
about them. What happened in recent centuries was not that
they were entirely forgotten but that they became divorced from
the general theology of grace. They still featured as part of
ascetical and mystical theology.[4] But without the underpinning
of an adequate theology of grace they became a rather esoteric
subject. The present 'revolution' arises from the realisation that
they are not peripheral but central in the daily living of the
ordinary Christian. So Christians must advert to their experiences of grace, they must appreciate and foster them, and must
learn to discern their meaning and act accordingly:

We shall not cease from exploration
And the end of all our exploring.
Will be to arrive where we started
And know the place for the first time.

T. S. Eliot: 'Little Gidding'

2. A THEOLOGICAL-SPIRITUAL JOURNEY

In the first part of this chapter I would like to recall some of the theological, pastoral, and religious influences which gradually led me to the understanding of the experience of grace which I outlined in the last chapter. This sharing of my journey may strike a chord in others and perhaps help them to articulate their religious experience in a way that is personally liberating. In the second part of the chapter I shall explain in more detail what the experience of grace entails.

I recall clearly the lessons we learned about sorrow for sin, in the primary school over thirty years ago. We were given various reasons for being sorry. But a lot of emphasis was laid on the point that sorrow for sin wasn't really a *feeling*. The teacher said that a person could be really sorry even without feeling sorry; and that feeling sorry was no guarantee that one really was sorry. Now this may have been merely a recognition that one's personal attitude is not to be equated simply with superficial emotions. But I strongly suspect that lurking behind it was the common teaching of the neo-scholastic theologians that the supernatural cannot be experienced.

Most of these theologians held that we could not have direct knowledge of the state of grace.[1] Nor could we be directly aware that an act of love was truly a supernatural act, 'because we cannot directly perceive its supernatural character'.[2] In support of their views they were able to refer to the writings of St Albert and St Bonaventure.[3] They even referred to St Thomas Aquinas —but generally speaking they did not do justice to the remarkably rich synthesis he had worked out.

It is generally said, and no doubt with a good deal of truth, that the reason why these authors banished grace to a realm beyond consciousness was because of the model they used to explain it. They envisaged a double-decker or two-tier structure, with a kind of higher nature (supernature) laid on top of human nature. The result is that they postulate a supernatural equivalent to such natural acts as knowing and willing. But this duplication applied only to strictly 'spiritual' acts; apparently it did not apply to feelings. Furthermore, they seem to have assumed that one could not be aware of the supernatural component in, say, an act of supernatural charity.

The neo-Scholastic model for understanding grace has come in for some harsh criticism recently. The criticism is justified in the case of the popularisers. But it may be that their main failure was that they did not take the model far enough. The creative theologian, Scheeben, on the other hand, works out the model with utter seriousness—and the result is that magnificent book *Nature and Grace,* first published in 1861 and well worthy of being translated into English nearly a hundred years later. He seems to suggest that the 'graced' person should be conscious of being in a supernatural state, through the employment of a set of supernaturalised faculties; the difficulty that arises is not that the supernatural is intrinsically beyond the reach of a 'graced' consciousness, but that it is only in heaven that 'supernature' will have integrated fully with nature.[4]

Rahner

Having been brought up on the popular neo-Scholastic theology of grace, I experienced it as something of a revelation to study, in the early 1960s, some articles on grace by Karl Rahner.[5] His analysis of the concept of nature was particularly interesting. It opened up a whole new range of theology by pointing out the inadequacy of the assumption that 'the natural' is that which can be known without the help of the Judaeo-Christian revelation. Rahner pointed out that all of world history is in fact oriented towards a supernatural destiny. So there is a supernatural aspect or element in what we think of as the natural world and secular history. This implies that it is not strictly accurate to use the phrase 'natural religion' to designate the great world religions or the traditional religion of tribal peoples. But it also has more personal, psychological, implications in regard to the possibility of experiencing grace.

One article by Rahner struck me particularly forcefully. It was a short piece entitled 'Reflections on the Experience of Grace'.[6] Let me quote from it:

> . . . have we ever experienced the *spiritual* in man? . . . Have we ever forgiven someone even when we got no thanks for it. . . . Have we ever been absolutely lonely? . . . Have we ever tried to love God when we seemed to be calling out into emptiness? . . . If we find such experiences, then we have experienced the spirit in the way meant here . . .

Having helped us to locate such experiences of spirit Rahner then goes on to apply his general theology of grace and the supernatural: '. . . once we experience the spirit in this way, we (at least, we as Christians who live in faith) have also already *in fact* experienced the *supernatural*. We have done so perhaps in a very anonymous and inexpressible manner.' Rahner's general position is that we do experience grace because the world we live in is actually and historically a 'graced' world. But within the kind of spiritual experiences he points to, we cannot draw a clear line of division between the purely natural component and the supernatural element.

This conclusion of Rahner's is important theologically. But what I think is more important in the long run is his attempt to bring theological terms back from the limbo of abstraction into which they had fallen and anchor them in personal human experience.

At this time I was doing research on the Protestant evangelical understanding of grace and salvation. Within this tradition there is one stream which lays great stress on spiritual feelings and especially the feeling of assurance that one has been accepted by God. In trying to correlate this with Catholic teaching I found that the binding doctrine of the Church was far less restrictive than the neo-Scholastic view. In fact the Council of Trent went to a great deal of trouble to allow for a plurality of theologies, condemning only the idea that one can be certain, with the certainty of a faith which does not allow for error, that one has been saved. I came to realise that there was the possibility of a far more positive approach by Catholics to spiritual feelings. And Jean Mouroux's book on *The Christian Experience* revealed what deep roots in tradition such an approach would have.[7]

In trying to promote a dialogue between Catholic and Protestant spiritualities I would have wished to work out some synthesis for myself. This would take seriously the theology of the supernatural, but it would also have to find room for an adequate account of spiritual feelings. I failed at that time to develop such a synthesis, probably because I was still too abstract in my approach to theology.

Existential theology

Three years later, two books by Rosemary Haughton (*On Trying to be Human* and *The Transformation of Man*)[8] offered the possibility of a far more existential style of theologising, which she describes as follows:

> You could call this experimental theology, but whatever name it is given the idea arose from the conviction that much theological discussion is wasted, not because the words used have no *possible* meaning but because the people who use them don't mean anything by them. They don't know what the words mean, even though they have almost certainly had precisely those experiences to which the words refer.[9]

I was really fascinated and excited, and this time the excitement was not purely intellectual; I was being challenged to discover in my daily secular experience the deep roots of the theological terms I had been throwing around for years. I didn't really get very far in the project. I think now that this was partly because I was still too rationalist in establishing the criteria for theological discussion and even for the meaning of theological terms. I think too that there wasn't sufficient depth in my experience to provide an adequate anchor for an existential meaning for words like 'grace'. What was particularly lacking was an adequate religious experience which would have provided a link between theological terms and overtly secular experiences of daily life.

Over a period of years I discovered, and allowed to develop, a more explicitly religious dimension to my life; and this eventually provided a basis for a more adequate understanding of grace. It came from a variety of sources, some theological and some pastoral. First of all I had to teach a theology course on providence. This forced me to take this primordial Christian belief very seriously, and to face up to its implications. I came to realise that it doesn't make much sense theologically to consider first the question of the existence of God and then go on to the question of his providence as a distinct problem. In fact the basic theological question (at least today) is whether there is some providence governing the pattern of the world. Having answered 'yes' to that question I can then give the name 'God' to that providence. Furthermore I cannot see much sense in trying to claim that there is providence in the major direction of the world's development but not in the little details; the only meaningful conception of providence I can affirm is one that is comprehensive, extending even to the numbering of the hairs on my head (*Luke* 12 : 7). Human freedom can still be safeguarded in such a theology of providence. In fact, so far as I can see, the centuries-old problem of reconciling God's sovereignty with human freedom has been solved—at least in its traditional theological form;[10] there remains, of course, the irreducible element of mystery which permeates every point where the Transcendent touches our lives.

Active pastoral involvement in a missionary situation opened up for me ranges and depths of religious experience which were new and exciting. Every day brought vivid illustrations of the liberating power of Christian faith in the lives of ordinary people. As a priest I could share in the religious experiences of my parishioners. And frequently I could play an active part in helping them to meet Christ or trust the Father or be guided by the Spirit.

The 'Charismatic Renewal' opened up further important aspects of spiritual experience. Especially important was the opportunity it gave for faith-sharing in small groups. It also taught me to pray spontaneously for people who felt oppressed by sickness or fear. This led to a considerable extension and deepening of my experience of grace.

A deeper theoretical and practical understanding of African traditional religion was a great help to me in understanding and appreciating religious experience. It tied in with the renewed theological interest over the past few years in the phenomenon of religion. There has been a reaction against the radically secular theology of a decade ago. Particularly helpful in this regard is the development of a new sociological approach to religion[11] which does not reduce religion to its purely social function, as earlier sociologists had attempted to do.

There has also been a remarkable development in the area of fundamental theology with a new appreciation of the fact that theology is essentially a reflection on religious experience.[12] This general theological interest in religion was heightened for me by a particular concern, as a missionary, with non-Christian religions. An attempt to discover the relationship between Christianity and the other religions cannot get very far if one remains on the level of theological concepts; one must get behind them to the living experience which they articulate.

Looking back on significant religious and theological influences which affected my understanding of grace, I think I should give an outstanding place to the renewal currently taking place in Ignatian spirituality. This involves getting back to what Ignatius Loyola really had in mind when he devised his famous spiritual exercises. For him spiritual feelings are of enormous importance. Indeed his whole approach to discernment presupposes and fosters an ability to be sensitive to our religious moods and feelings.[13] This is integral to his spirituality of 'finding God in all things'. When I speak of faith as the ability to see God in all things, I am adapting this phrase of Ignatius. His use of the word 'finding' puts the stress on the active search for the will of God. By using the word 'see' I am stressing a different, but complementary, aspect, namely, the givenness of faith, the fact that in a sense it is prior to my activity.

A depth-experience

Having outlined the background to my present approach to the experience of grace it may be appropriate at this stage to give a concrete instance of the more personalist type of theology it involves. Quite recently many people whom I know have been enormously encouraged, enlightened and comforted by reading an article called 'Enigma and Tenderness' by Kevin O'Shea. It seemed to touch some deep point in the experience of people of widely different temperament and background. What he describes seems to me to be a very good instance of what might be an experience of grace. Briefly, he points to a deeply human experience we have of an element of alienation and incorrigible inhumanness and restlessness in the very core of our being; this is what he calls the experience of 'enigma'. We cannot cope with it either by fighting it or by running away from it. But we can experience a healing and a sense of wholeness through what he calls the way of tenderness, mediated through warm affective relationships:

> When a person knows this tenderness within him, he is less afraid to get close to the pain and hurt within him. He can come quite near. He will not fight or deny it. He can take a good soft look at it. . . . Somehow there is a moment of 'recognition', a moment in which he can distance himself from his pain to look at it closely and calmly, but a moment in which he can claim it and own it as his, and not be overwhelmed by the fact that it is as it is and has always been. There is a recognition of frailty that is constructive, and creative, and integrative for the person: it heals. . . . It is like ceasing to be as he formerly had to be to cope . . . it is an ability to let it go, to be joyfully at calm peace in it, though it is not of one's own making. Perhaps one's whole being is touched, and responds.[14]

In a subsequent article[15] O'Shea probes further and unveils an element of continuing isolation and restlessness which may well come to consciousness and even be heightened by the healing experience of tenderness: '. . . there is, it would seem, *the birth of a new loneliness*.'[16] His account of this can supply the concrete detail we need if we are to breathe real life into Augustine's classic claim that our hearts are restless until they rest in God.

As a style of theologising, this approach of O'Shea's seems to me to be very close to that of Kierkegaard. Take for instance this moving passage in which Kierkegaard speaks of the concept of dread:

> . . . he who . . . remains with dread . . . does not recoil . . . but

B

he bids it welcome . . . as Socrates solemnly flourished the poisoned goblet . . . he says, as a patient says to the surgeon when a painful operation is about to begin, 'Now I am ready.' Then dread enters into his soul and searches it thoroughly, constraining out of him all the finite and the petty, and leading him hence whither he would go. . . . With the help of faith dread trains the individual to find repose in providence . . . he who has truly learned to be in dread will tread as in a dance when the dreads of finiteness strike up their tune, and the disciples of finiteness lose their wits and their courage.[17]

O'Shea points out that a major element in the new loneliness of which he speaks is the sense of guilt. He explains: 'It is not so much guilt about any particular thing . . . as guilt about the whole existential situation that now obtains.'[18] This seems to echo the remarks of Kierkegaard: 'So also it is with regard to guilt, which is the second thing dread discovers. . . . He . . . who only learns to recognise his guilt by analogy with the decisions of the police justice or the supreme court never really comprehends that he is guilty; for if a man is guilty, he is infinitely guilty.'[19]

Religious experience

It is probably better to use the term 'depth-experience' than 'religious experience' for the kind of thing that Kierkegaard and O'Shea are describing. There is a religious dimension in the experience but it may be more or less latent. In order to bring it to the surface one can attempt a special kind of interpretation which uncovers the religious aspects or implications of the experience.[20] This is basically a theological operation, a part of the new fundamental theology which we need today. The approach is by way of some common denominator, some vaguely religious dimension of life common to all religions and even to the authentic agnostic or atheist; this needs to be 'unfolded' into something like explicit Christianity.

There is another, and more practical, way of bringing out the religious dimension of depth-experiences of the kind described. It is to become more explicitly religious oneself, consciously to allow Christian faith to permeate every facet of one's life. In this way every peak-experience will be apprehended within the context of an all-embracing religious awareness. The religious dimensions will no longer be latent but will become more and more explicit. A fervent Hindu will articulate and even apprehend depth-experiences within the framework of the Hindu religious outlook. Correspondingly, a Christian whose life is steeped in prayer will discover a very explicit Christianity in experiences that for somebody else might be only implicitly religious. It is then that we can speak properly of religious experience, and even of a Christian experience.

Spill-over effect

Without some kind of depth-experiences the Christian life will be thin and superficial. Indeed one could hardly speak of a genuine Christian experience unless it is anchored in something really deep such as an experience of contingency, or loneliness, or guilt, or participation in an ultimate reality. But once such experiences do occur in a Christian context there can be what I would call a spill-over effect or a feed-back effect which results in very ordinary experiences of daily life becoming profoundly religious events. If, as a result of an experience of contingency, I come to find 'repose in providence' (to quote from the passage of Kierkegaard given above) then this experience of being in the hands of a loving, provident Father can permeate every moment of life. Indeed one of the most exciting and moving experiences one can have is to find that some trivial item of daily life has become the occasion of a personal encounter with the Father, with Christ the Lord, or with the Holy Spirit. To meet God in the depth-experience is almost what one would expect; but to find that he awaits us in the insignificant details adds an element of graciousness, of magnanimity, of eagerness and above all of freedom, to the encounter. For instance: that God should answer *important* prayers is a proof that he is God. That he should choose to answer *minor* ones is almost beyond belief— and to experience it makes one want to shout for joy. It liberates us from pomposity, from taking even our prayer too seriously. Without denying the tragic character of the world we live in, it gently spins it on its axis to reveal it as also a 'divine comedy'. It gives the credibility of experienced truth to the words of the gospel:

> I tell you, do not be anxious about your life, what you shall eat or what you shall drink, nor about your body, what you shall put on. . . . Look at the birds of the air . . . your heavenly Father feeds them. Are you not of more value than they? (*Matt.* 6:25-26).
>
> I tell you, my friends, do not fear those who kill the body. . . . Are not five sparrows sold for two pennies? And not one of them is forgotten before God. Why, even the hairs of your head are all numbered. Fear not; you are of more value than many sparrows. (*Luke* 12:4-7).

Supernatural

It is against this background that I say that grace now means for me God making himself personally present to me in a variety of ways. It may be in a depth-experience or it may be in some trivial event of life which, in virtue of what I called the 'feed-back effect', has become in fact a reminder of the wider context of my life. But in either case there is a personal encounter with the provident Father or with Christ the Saviour or with the life-giving Spirit.

I understand this grace to be strictly supernatural. And I would interpret this primarily in terms of the revelation of God as Father, Son and Spirit. The events of my daily life as actually experienced by me can be instances of the self-revelation of God. And not merely self-revelation but self-communication; for it is in making himself present in my life that God reveals himself to me. To be in living contact with the Father, Son, and Spirit seems to be beyond anything that is strictly owed to me as human. So I can say it involves an intrinsic change in me. This change might be conceived of in Scholastic terms as 'sanctifying grace' in its created aspect. But other conceptualisations or interpretations of the change might be equally satisfactory (and unsatisfactory!). What is important is that the focus is not taken off the self-communication of God. To put it in Scholastic terms, we must not allow uncreated grace (God present in us and to us) to take second place to created grace (an intrinsic change in the person).[21]

This approach leaves one with the problem of explaining how those who have no contact with Christian revelation can in fact receive supernatural grace. But this problem is much the same as is met by any theology which accepts the need for supernatural revelation. However, in the approach suggested here the problem of supernatural *grace* is linked more obviously to that of supernatural *revelation*. Modern theology has gone quite a long way towards a solution to the problem. The most significant step is the realisation that one should stop thinking in terms of a logical process by which what is implicit becomes explicit, and begin instead to uncover and interpret what is latent in the actual living out of life, as I suggested.

The points made in the past two paragraphs are meant merely as an indication that it is possible to speak of experiencing grace without compromising the notion of the supernatural. I should add, however, that it would be a mistake, and probably impossible in any case, to try to fit every aspect of a theology of experienced grace into the confines of the neo-Scholastic framework;[22] but it is necessary to safeguard the basic points these theologians were defending, especially the gratuitousness of grace. I do not propose here to work out a detailed theology of grace as an experienced reality. What I have said on the topic so far, and some further points which I shall make in chapter 6, are intended merely as a background for a much more practical treatment of the experience of grace. There are more personal and urgent questions facing each of us than what it *means* to experience grace. Such questions are: Do I *in fact* have such experiences? If not, how can I get into a state or situation where I can do so? If I do already have such an experience, how can I foster it and derive maximum benefit from it?

The remainder of this book is chiefly concerned with these existential questions. This does not mean that it will attempt to offer practical guidelines on how to promote religious experiences of all kinds in one's life. My aim is more modest. It is to throw some light on the spirituality of those groups of Christians who make the most spectacular claims to religious experience—

namely, the Pentecostalists and those involved in the Charismatic Renewal. I shall focus attention on the outstanding and dramatic experience which plays a dominant role in their spirituality, and in the lives of most of them. This is the religious experience called (by them) 'baptism in the Spirit'. By offering an assessment of its meaning and value I hope to promote a fruitful dialogue between traditional Christian spirituality and the Pentecostal spirituality which has come to play an increasingly important part in Christianity today.

PART TWO

A NEW HEART

3. BAPTISM IN THE SPIRIT AS A RELIGIOUS EXPERIENCE

Many people in the various Christian Churches maintain that they have undergone a remarkable religious experience which has changed the pattern and quality of their lives. What has happened to them, they say, is basically the same as what happened to the followers of Jesus at the first Pentecost. So these Christians of today describe their own experience in the words used in Scripture to refer to Pentecost: they say they have been 'baptised with the Holy Spirit' (*Acts* 1:5) and they usually call the experience 'baptism in the Spirit'.

In this chapter I would like to look closely at the experience they describe. I think there are certain advantages in prescinding entirely at first from what is meant in Scripture by being 'baptised in the Spirit' and asking simply what this religious experience means today for those who claim to have undergone it. A helpful way to do this is to relate it to the conversion experiences common in Evangelical Protestantism.

A conversion?

For the past eighty years the psychology of conversion has been a favourite subject of study for psychologists.[1] Most of them have been interested almost exclusively in the *pattern* of the experience of people who were converted in a dramatic way. These people had felt troubled, lost and oppressed. Then they experienced a breakthrough to a new world of freedom and peace. As the hymn 'Amazing Grace' puts it: 'I once was lost, but now am found,/Was blind, but now can see.' Concentrating on this pattern of feelings, most of the psychologists paid little attention to the meaning or interpretation given to the experience by the convert. As far as these empirical psychologists were concerned it mattered little whether the person was being converted to God or to some atheistic ideology.

A psychologist of this kind, listening to the typical testimony of people who describe how they were baptised in the Spirit, would simply say that this was a conversion-experience. The pattern is very much the same—a breakthrough from bondage to a world of peace, light, freedom and joy. If the psychologist has a reductionist approach, regarding the feelings alone as significant, then it will be considered a matter of no great consequence that these people interpret their experience in terms rather different from those used by other converts—and that strict Pentecostalists see their being baptised in the Spirit as a 'second blessing', something distinct from conversion to Christian faith.

In this study I hope to adopt a psychological approach which avoids the kind of reductionism just described. I believe that the *meaning* of the experience called 'baptism in the Spirit' is itself an integral part of the experience. So we shall be concerned not merely with a description of feelings but with discerning the meaning of the whole experience.

The first point to note is that the experience in question does not always mean exactly what the person who undergoes it thinks it means.[2] That may seem to be an odd or even a paradoxical statement. I shall go to some trouble to explain it because the explanation is a key to a proper understanding of 'baptism in the Spirit'. And such an understanding is in turn the key to a reconciliation of Pentecostal spirituality with that of the mainstream Christian tradition.

Intrinsic and imposed meaning

I would like to propose a distinction between what we can call 'intrinsic meaning' and 'imposed meaning'. The distinction can be illustrated by considering a very well-documented historical case, namely, the conversion-experience undergone by John Wesley in 1738. The special relevance of this case is that in many respects it was very close to the experience called 'baptism in the Spirit' nowadays—yet it was interpreted by Wesley himself in a rather different sense—in fact in *two* different senses.

John Wesley had been an earnest, sincere and dedicated

Christian clergyman for several years before he had his conversion-experience. He came in contact with a group of extremely evangelical people called Moravian Brethren. They convinced him that he was not a true Christian because he had not been 'converted'. After months of doubt and spiritual anguish he eventually had his conversion-experience, on a day which one would have to call the birthday of Methodism. During and immediately after the experience Wesley interpreted it in the strict Moravian sense, as 'being saved' through a rebirth from sin to grace—in fact to sinlessness. But before long he began to qualify this very simple position. He felt obliged to do this because he found that his post-conversion experience did not really fit the pattern too well. For instance the assurance of being in God's favour, which was to have been the most obvious and certain sign of being saved, turned out to be somewhat intermittent; at times it was strong, at other times it seemed to be absent or very nearly so. Wesley was both a good theologian and a keen practical religious psychologist. He was constantly analysing his own religious experience and that of his many converts, trying always to correlate theory with the actual experience. As the years went by he modified his interpretation of his conversion. He always preserved the central point that one is saved by the grace of God, received in faith. But on almost every other point his later understanding of his conversion diverged from the strict Moravian view which he had first held.[3] For instance he came to recognise that after his 'conversion' he was still not fully free of sin. He even accepted that before his conversion he was not really 'lost' in the strict theological sense.

We can now consider how the categories of *intrinsic* and *imposed* meaning apply to Wesley's experience—and how his experience illustrates what these terms mean. First, in regard to his experience just prior to conversion: I would say that its *intrinsic* meaning was a sense of being powerless in the face of sin, of being oppressed by his own sinfulness, of not being given over to God, of being lost (in some way that cannot be specified precisely). The *imposed* meaning of this experience was that he was in a 'state of sin', deserving of damnation; this imposed meaning was later watered down and practically qualified out of existence. Secondly, in regard to the conversion itself: I think the *intrinsic* meaning was the immersion in God's forgiving love, the unmerited breaking by God of the weight and power of sin (to some undetermined extent), the gifts of freedom, peace and assurance, and the opening up of a deeper, richer relationship with God. The *imposed* meaning of the conversion was rebirth to a new and sinless nature, the elimination of all trace of sin, and the conviction that the Spirit had been given in a way that would never allow a moment's doubt of God's favour. Wesley later modified this imposed meaning, giving a more qualified sense to the key terms.

The difference

The crucial point emerging from this analysis is that the intrinsic meaning of Wesley's experience remains the same even when he changes the imposed meaning. The reason is that the intrinsic meaning is a built-in part of the experience itself. The imposed meaning on the other hand is an interpretation added on from outside the experience. The experience is open to a variety of imposed meanings or interpretations.

Does this lead to the conclusion that the imposed meaning is quite unimportant? Not at all. The imposed meaning has its own importance because it is the way in which the person situates this particular experience within the wider context of his or her current belief-system or outlook. For instance, as we have seen, Wesley interpreted his conversion-experience differently at different stages of his life, modifying his interpretation in accordance with the changes in his theological outlook. And of course one of the main reasons why he changed his theology was precisely because his earlier one could not easily accommodate his experience. This is a good example of how the imposed meaning can be seen as an attempt to correlate a person's general theology or outlook with a given concrete experience.

A theological model

Quite rightly Wesley gave priority to the facts of his experience over his previously-held theory. This is what any theologian (or indeed any scientist) must do; and we shall try to do it in examining the experience called 'baptism in the Spirit'. But it may be well to note here that even the facts of experience are not entirely independent of theory. We do not enter any experience 'red raw'. Our general outlook gives us certain expectations, certain priorities in what to look for and what to value, certain categories of thought and modes of feeling. And all of these come into play in our experience. So even the intrinsic meaning of an experience is moulded to a considerable extent by our outlook. This means that in practice the difference between intrinsic and imposed meaning may not be nearly so clear as I have suggested above. Nevertheless the distinction can be very helpful. We can think of it as a theological model, a way of highlighting two aspects of meaning. By deliberately applying the model we can analyse any religious experience far more accurately, distinguishing intrinsic from imposed elements in what would otherwise be an undifferentiated whole.

It is time now to turn directly to the contemporary situation and attempt to discern the nature and significance of the experience known as baptism in the Spirit. Is it something that should happen to every Christian? If so, does it necessarily take the form of a dramatic breakthrough? How does it relate to infant baptism? Is it the same thing as the conversion which Evangelical Christians believe is the real beginning of Christian life? Is it the same thing as is referred to in Scripture as 'being baptised in the Spirit'? The key to finding an answer to these questions is to distinguish the intrinsic meaning from the imposed meaning of the experience. We must consider what has actually happened to people who claim to have been baptised in the Spirit, and try to disentangle this from the various interpretations given of it. We must try to see if people who make no claim to have been baptised in the Spirit may in fact have had similar experiences, interpreted differently and going under a different name, or perhaps no name at all.

Intrinsic meaning of baptism in the Spirit

The following is a list of certain common features which seem to me to be intrinsic to the experience of a large number of people who say they have been baptised in the Spirit. They have a sense of breakthrough into a new world where they feel totally accepted, cherished and loved by an unlimited love. They experience an overwhelming sense of being set free from sinful selfishness and frequently from some specific attitude or habit of sin which had oppressed them. Consequently, they feel a deep interior peace. They feel that they have 'come alive inside' and they now experience a rich range of religious emotions ranging from the gift of tears (in many cases) to a deep joy. This liberation of the emotions is not confined to the specifically religious area but extends right through daily living and is especially evident in a new openness to others and an ability to trust them and share with them at a deep level. It is not uncommon for this to be associated with an inner healing of some old psychological hurts which had blocked the person's spiritual freedom and development. A very significant part of the experience is a real thirst for prayer and above all a desire to praise God; the gift of tongues which is often part of the experience or follows on it, is experienced as a gift of prayer—one has the sense of a power greater than oneself praying with and in one. The desire and the courage to pray with others may begin, or increase considerably, in this experience. This whole range of new abilities and attitudes and sensations is experienced as an undeserved and surprising gift; this *sense of gift* is one of the most significant and typical features of all.

To list the various features of the experience as we have just done may give the impression that all these are diverse items with little intrinsic connection between them. But in fact they are experienced as springing from one source and forming a coherent unity. So it is generally found that they do not come one at a time. The person who experiences one of them seems to become open to experiencing all, at least in some degree; though it may take some time to notice the full extent of what has happened. Because the different aspects are linked together there is often a sense of a definite breakthrough which is very memorable since it initiates intense religious awareness over a whole range of conscious life.

New relations with Father, Son and Spirit

What we have described so far might perhaps be summed up

as an entirely new and living relationship with God. But it should
be noted that in many cases there is question of something far
more specific than a relationship with God-in-general. Rather
there is the experience of a new relationship with one or all of
the three persons of the Trinity. There may be a vivid sense of
the *Father* watching every action, listening to every prayer, an-
ticipating every need. There may be a feeling that *Christ* has
become real, that one has met him, that he has become the Lord
of one's daily life. There may be a sense of the *Spirit* praying
within, guiding the person even in the minor choices of every
day, and at times inspiring the person to speak in his name. These
specifically Trinitarian experiences are not shared by everybody
who claims to have been baptised in the Spirit—at least not
very overtly or vividly. In a particular case all or some or
none of them may be present. At times one of these new
relationships is experienced so vividly that the others are scarcely
adverted to, at least at first. For instance an individual may
have that sense of being in living contact with Christ which is
so vividly expressed in the prayer called St Patrick's Breast-
plate:

. . . Christ with me, Christ within me
. . . Christ to comfort and restore me,
Christ in quiet, Christ in danger,
Christ in hearts of all that love me,
Christ in mouth of friend or stranger.

Are these new relationships to be considered as part of the
intrinsic meaning of baptism in the Spirit? I would reply that
they lie on the boundary-line between the intrinsic and the imposed meanings, sharing something of each. This vivid awareness
of the Father, of Jesus as Lord and of the Spirit are concrete
ways in which the love, care, guidance, power, mercy and providence of God are experienced. These particular expressions are
due to the influence of the whole Christian tradition and particularly to the specific contribution of the pentecostal-charismatic spirituality which lays so much stress on these aspects of
our Christian faith. As I said earlier, the tradition moulds the
expectation of the person and the categories of thought and
modes of feeling into which the intrinsic meaning of the experi-

ence is channelled and in which it is expressed. So we can say that the experience of God's providence and merciful love is the deepest core of the intrinsic meaning of baptism in the Spirit. But this frequently finds a concrete and vivid expression in the sense of the care of the Father, the Lordship of Jesus Christ and the power and guidance of the Holy Spirit.

Imposed meaning

People who undergo the experience of being baptised in the Spirit naturally try to relate it to a general theology or spirituality. So they interpret the experience, *imposing* a meaning on it. It may never occur to them that this further meaning is not really intrinsic to the experience. But that this is so becomes clear when we find that there may be a variety of different imposed meanings all of which are compatible with the intrinsic meaning. In this sense, baptism in the Spirit may mean something rather different to a classic Pentecostalist, to a strict Evangelical Protestant, to a Catholic in the Ignatian tradition of spirituality, to a Catholic involved in the Charismatic Renewal, and to any Christian who has been taught to distrust deep feelings, at least in religious matters.

To evaluate the strengths and weaknesses of various interpretations we must consider the extent to which each of them does justice to the intrinsic meaning of the experience and at the same time fits in with the overall Christian outlook and teaching as articulated in Scripture and tradition. So let us briefly consider some possible interpretations:

1. The experience may be dismissed as mere emotion and therefore unimportant. But this is to overlook its lasting significance in the lives of many Christians.

2. It may be interpreted as a 'consolation' in the Ignatian sense. This is quite correct but it does not go far enough. One needs to give greater weight to the fact that it initiates a new type of Christian experience for the person.

3. One can interpret the experience in the strict Pentecostal way as a second blessing, distinct from conversion. But this is to misunderstand the New Testament outlook. There is no real basis in Scripture for such a two-tier conception of

Christian life. In fact the accounts of Christian faith in the New Testament support the view that the normal Christian experience in those times included the features we have listed above as typical of the person who today claims to have been baptised in the Spirit. (We shall discuss this in chapter 5.)

4. There is the strictly 'Evangelical' Protestant view that anybody whose faith does not have the features listed above (deep peace, joy, etc.) is not really a Christian at all. So what others call 'baptism in the Spirit' may well be thought of by Evangelicals as the person's *first* conversion—at least in cases where prior to this the person had no deep or evident Christian experience.

Prima facie, there is strong scriptural support for this fourth view. It raises for us the basic issue whether, or in what sense, baptism in the Spirit is a requirement of any real Christian faith.

We can agree with the Evangelicals that a person who is converted to Christ from a life of sinful unbelief should normally have a vivid sense of entering into a new world of forgiveness, freedom and peace. But to adopt the strict Evangelical view that anybody who has not had such a decisive experience of entering a new world cannot be a Christian at all, is to set oneself against the tradition of the main Christian Churches. It is also to play down the difference between coming to the faith as an adult convert (as New Testament Christians did) and growing up in and into the faith (as most Christians do today). While not accepting the extreme Evangelical view of the minimum requirements of faith, I find it very helpful because it provokes us into calling in question the usual presuppositions about what is normal for a Christian.

Asking the right questions

Out of such a perspective we can begin to ask the right questions about baptism in the Spirit. An allegory may illustrate how we might be led astray by failing to ask the right questions. Suppose there were an unsuspected poison in almost every kind of food so that nearly everybody was chronically sick. Looking at the lucky few who were not poisoned, people might well ask:

'What is the special gift they have been given and what does it add to "normal" human nature?' These questions are misleading. The questions that need to be asked are: 'What prevents the majority from living a truly normal human life and how can normality be restored to them?' Applying the allegory we suggest that it is misleading to ask: 'What is *added* to the normal Christian when he is baptised in the Spirit, and is this addition something new (a "second blessing") or merely a release or manifestation of something present already?' Such questions tend to accept as the norm a kind of Christian life which differs considerably from the New Testament norms.

It is more helpful to ask the following questions. What is the dimension that is *absent* from the lives of so many Christians today, leaving them so different from the Christians of New Testament times? What kind of Christian life, if any, remains when this is absent? How did Christians ever come to accept such an impoverished kind of Christian life as the norm? And what must take place in order that a Christian today should come to share the kind of experience that is characteristic of really normal Christian living? Is it perhaps by undergoing the experience which is nowadays called 'baptism in the Spirit'? And this leads on to questions about what forms such an experience can take, and whether there is a danger that some people or groups might be inclined to 'canonise' just one form and play down other equally valid forms.

The missing dimension

Our answer to the first of these questions is that the dimension absent from the lives of many Christians today is the conscious experience of being in the hands of a redemptive and loving providence, made visible in Christ and brought home to them from moment to moment by the Holy Spirit. Providence and redemption are accepted by ordinary Christians as fundamental doctrines, part of their belief-system. But whereas other doctrines have permeated the feelings of ordinary Christians, providence and redemption find little or no echo in the deep spontaneous attitudes of such people. Most Christians do really feel the truth of the Church's teaching about the goodness of creation, about the reality and power of personal and social sin, about the duty to work to better the world and to help others, about the brotherhood of man and the values of truth and justice. They may not always live up to their beliefs and their best instincts on these issues, but when they fail to do so they experience a feeling of inauthenticity or guilt. But the situation is quite different in regard to the Christian teaching that each one of us is saved from evil and is lovingly cared for by God at every instant of our lives —so that redemption and providence are not two separate truths but are linked in an extraordinary synthesis of nature and grace. This part of the Christian outlook doesn't seem to have sunk into the depths of the psyche of the ordinary Christian—those depths from which spontaneous reactions, attitudes and sentiments emerge. The result is that even where the Christian message is taught in a correct and balanced way it is often understood in an unbalanced way by the hearers; the aspect that does not echo their spontaneous convictions is felt to be peripheral and less credible. And the neglected dimension is the lived experience of being dependent from moment to moment on a caring and saving God.

Even preachers and teachers are liable to have assimilated Christianity in this watered-down form. This leads to an imbalance in their presentation of the message. They will lay too little stress on the aspect whose truth and validity they have not felt deeply and the same distortion may be present in the witness given by their lives. As a result, ordinary Christians may be largely deprived of a presentation of the Christian outlook on redemption and providence that has the right emphasis and conviction.

This process of distortion is part of the answer to one of the key questions posed earlier, namely, how did Christians ever come to accept such an impoverished kind of Christianity as the norm? But we must add that the distortion was greatly aggravated by various historical factors which we can only briefly touch upon.[4] In a world where nearly everybody accepted Christian teaching, its strangeness was less obvious; and where people were reared as Christians from childhood they were less likely to experience the full force of its wonder. In this atmosphere there could develop the tendency to envisage Christianity as a belief-system, a morals-system and a cult-system. Conformity to these systems could be taken as the criterion by which to judge who is a normal Christian. Large numbers of purely nominal Christians dragged down the criterion further. The excesses of enthusiasts alienated respectable Christians and led to suspicion of the experiential dimensions of religion. The prevailing rationalism and voluntarism of recent centuries reinforced this attitude. Then there is the perennial 'foolishness' at the heart of Christian faith, the child-like simplicity which eludes the self-important. And finally we must mention the difficulty that Christians, and the Church itself, always have in really taking seriously the 'freedom of the Spirit'; it is so much easier and safer to fall back on law in one form or another, not trusting oneself, or others, or the Spirit. Having eliminated the reality of Spirit-led freedom, people may retain the terminology, and even imagine that they are experiencing the freedom of the Gospel.

Are they Christians?

We turn now to face the question, posed with great force by extreme evangelicals, whether this kind of impoverished Christian life merits the name Christian faith at all. To answer this, let us try to discover what is left when the vivid conviction of being redeemed and cared for is missing. The extreme Evangelical is wrong in claiming that only a purely nominal Christianity is left; one can see this by looking at the lives of so many faithful and dutiful Christians who lack this special dimension of the faith. What remains to them is a world-view, including a belief-system and a set of values, which at its best can commit a person to dedicated service of others and dutiful service of God.

But this service will be experienced as a costly one, by no means an 'easy yoke and a light burden'. Such a Christian is earnest, diligent, calculating, painstaking; what is lacking is a certain spontaneity, joy and light-hearted enthusiasm in the person's service of God and others. The category of duty is dominant. Even prayer (perhaps especially prayer!) is something one ought to do rather than something one wants to do. The difference between the two states is typified in the different meanings given to the phrase, 'I hope it will work out well.' For the ordinary Christian this means that the outcome is left open. He or she feels or fears that things may in fact turn out badly. Of course such people dutifully accept that God has our interests at heart and that he can do what he wills. But they scarcely think of invoking such beliefs in this instance; their acceptance of these truths is rather notional. For the other kind of Christian, hope is a conviction, a firm confidence, that things really will work out for the best, even if not in quite the way we would like at present. It is based not on the intrinsic probabilities of the situation but on a total trust in a transcendent and personal providence. This conviction will generally include a strong feeling of confidence; but it is not just a feeling, for at times it is a conviction based on naked faith, unsupported by feeling, and perhaps even in spite of a contrary feeling.

Are they saved?

In the absence of this kind of hope, in the absence of abiding Christian joy and of experienced freedom, many good Christians find themselves weighed down by responsibilities, harassed by worries and fears, almost immobilised by a sense of helplessness and insecurity, oppressed by an almost compulsive sense of duty or by a partly neurotic feeling of guilt, and isolated by an inability to trust others. The extreme Evangelical view is that such people have not been 'saved'. Can we deny that there is a large measure of truth in this judgment? What right have we to define 'being saved' in a way that bears little or no relation to its existential meaning? Not that we should limit salvation to an experienced sense of liberation. Neither Evangelical nor Catholic would wish to do that. There are important moral, social and eschatological dimensions to salvation as well. But must we not admit that the salvation of such a troubled Christian is as yet a very partial one? We may not agree with the all-or-nothing judgment of the Evangelical. But equally we must admit the weakness of an all-or-nothing 'Catholic' version which explains salvation in terms of an unexperienceable ontological reality and considers the daily experience of the person as quite accidental or irrelevant. The only way forward seems to be to drop the crude simplicities of both traditions and face the fact that *Christian salvation has many dimensions which, despite their intrinsic links with each other, are to some extent separable in this life.* All of these dimensions are important, even essential; and not least is the experienced dimension of personal liberation.

What is this change?

And so we move on to the most crucial of all the questions we posed earlier: what must take place in order that a Christian today should come to share in the kind of experience which is characteristic of truly normal Christianity? Here the normal is determined not by statistics but by considering what is intrinsic to Christian faith, especially as it is found in the New Testament. To give an adequate and concrete answer to this question one would need to consider two distinct aspects—the individual and the social. The social aspect involves important considerations about the role which a group can play in the process; these would require a fairly extended treatment which we must bypass here. We shall concentrate on the individual aspect, trying to pinpoint what is the psychological and spiritual change that takes place in a person in the experience called 'baptism in the Spirit' —or in any experience which has the same intrinsic meaning, even though it may go by a different name, or be given no name at all.

What then is the decisive change which takes place when the usual earnest type of Christian becomes a truly normal Christian in the proper sense? Our answer is that the crucial factor is a change by which the Christian faith which governs a person's *deliberate* consciousness has now found deep echoes in the area of *spontaneous* consciousness.

To explain what this means we must note that in the adult human there are several levels of conscious and non-conscious life. At the 'top' is the level of deliberate consciousness where the ego thinks and decides. 'Below' that there is a level of spontaneous consciousness, where immediate reactions and attitudes are generated. These spontaneous reactions can be resisted by conscious effort. They can also be modified to some extent by the deliberate development of different attitudes. For instance, somebody who is spontaneously hasty and impatient may deliberately act slowly and patiently and may try to let calmness permeate the spontaneous level of consciousness. 'Below' the level of spontaneous consciousness is a level of reflexes at the psycho-motor level. These are pre-conscious. Nevertheless they can be deliberately conditioned to react in specific ways. 'Below' that level again is a level of biological-chemical reactions. These condition the 'higher' levels (as we discover when we see somebody who is drunk or drugged or whose endocrine glands are not working properly); but they do not entirely determine the person's conscious behaviour.

A new heart

God is operative in the constitution and activity of every level of human activity; to accept that is part of the Christian belief in providence. And in the present order this is not a merely 'natural' providence; it is redemptive in the full supernatural sense. So the grace of God is working in the life of a child long before that child can respond freely; the responses of infancy are at a level where consciousness is as yet inchoate and emergent. As the higher levels of consciousness develop, God's grace becomes operative there. The Christian child learns to speak to God by saying prayers and learns to listen to God and obey him by accepting the teaching of those who claim to speak in his name. For many adults, perhaps for most, this is what it means to live consciously as a Christian. Faith for them is located in this area of deliberate consciousness.

The change that occurs in the case of somebody baptised in the Spirit is that the person's deliberate faith now seems to find an extraordinary resonance at the level of spontaneous consciousness. Prior to this, one had prayed deliberately, offered oneself deliberately to God, consciously tried to allow the Word of God to guide one's thoughts, decisions and actions. All this must be called a presence of God in consciousness, even an experience of God's grace. But in and after the change, all that the person had been trying to do *deliberately* seems somehow to happen *spontaneously*.

In chapter 7 I shall explore in some detail the psychological aspect of this change and its cause; and I shall draw out the implications for a theology of faith. But here it is better to remain at the descriptive level.

The change that takes place is not primarily a *moral* one, enabling the person to succeed now in doing what he or she had been failing to do previously—though that may happen in some matters. Rather it is that the person's spontaneous consciousness seems suffused with the presence of God. That is why people speak of feeling 'a fountain of joy' or 'a deep spring of hope' or 'an ocean of peace and freedom' and so on. There is the sense of life bubbling up—and according to our interpretation this is the life of the spontaneous reactions, feelings and attitudes which have now been transformed by the grace and power of God. There is nothing new in the fact that feelings and images bubble up into immediate consciousness; for that is the way our consciousness works all the time. What is new is the changed *content* of this material that emerges. Attitudes and 'affects' of fear, suspicion, self-interest, hopelessness and worry—together with the images which carry such emotions—seem to be very largely replaced by joy, hope, trust, openness, love and peace— and by the kind of images which can carry this new affective material.

This account may perhaps give the impression that the person baptised in the Spirit lives constantly in a state of peak experience. Indeed some testimonies do suggest this. In some cases at least the person does seem to live on a religious 'high' for weeks or even months. But the sense of God's loving presence varies in intensity even during this honeymoon period. And almost everybody will admit to going through a 'low' sooner or later. Nevertheless this is seldom experienced as simply a return to the earlier situation. Even in aridity or darkness the person feels that something more or less irreversible has occurred. The blocks that prevented faith from reaching into the centre of affectivity have been removed. A whole new area of conscious life has been opened up to the grace of God. Consequently, even the absence of God in one's feelings can now be experienced as a real grace; it is no longer something purely negative but an emptiness crying out for fulfilment, a void that makes one hunger and thirst for God.

The basis for this new kind of experience of God seems to be a deeply rooted conviction of being totally accepted and cherished by God. It is a conviction that is not just in the head but above all in the heart—that is, in the seat of the affective life. The person experiences this as an utterly unmerited gift, an outpouring of love which removes 'the heart of stone' that had been so cold and insensitive to God and to others. The works of Ezekiel's prophecy seem very apt to describe the change:

> I shall give you a new heart,
> and put a new spirit in you;
> I shall remove the heart of stone from your bodies
> and give you a heart of flesh instead.
>
> *Ezek.* 36:26

To be baptised in the Spirit is, then, to have been given 'a new heart' and 'a new spirit', so that the sense of the redeeming love of God has permeated one's spontaneous feelings. So what is in question is primarily a state rather than a single event. For this reason it is preferable to speak of being baptised in the Spirit rather than of baptism in the Spirit; for the latter phrase suggests an event while the former one can indicate an enduring state. Of course it is more or less inevitable that people will want to speak at times of baptism in the Spirit as an event. That is fine provided it is recognised that the importance of the event is that it is the beginning of the state. Just as the primary meaning of 'marriage' must be the state of being married rather than simply the wedding-ceremony, so the primary meaning of being 'baptised in the Spirit' is the state rather than the event or process which initiates it.

Sudden or gradual

There is a very important conclusion to be drawn from what has just been said. It is that from a theological point of view there is no *a priori* reason why the state of being baptised in the Spirit should have to begin with a sudden and dramatic breakthrough. *It is just as important, and just as much the free gift of God, if it comes more slowly.* The form in which the gift comes is more a matter of the psychology of the person than of theology.

Entry into this new state commonly occurs in one of three different forms or patterns which we can call 'the dramatic pattern', 'the delayed-action pattern' and 'the cumulative pattern'. The dramatic pattern is the one which all in the Pentecostal tradition, including people of the Charismatic Renewal, tend to adopt as the ideal. The breakthrough occurs as the person is being prayed over. The person seems to yield, almost at times to dissolve, as a great pressure is released and peace and freedom flood the heart. It is not unusual for this to be very emotional and convulsive. There is not any doubt that such a sudden and dramatic breakthrough can be of great help, and of lasting significance, for many people who experience it. It makes the entry into a new state very memorable. The strong emotions of the experience can continue to re-echo in the person's consciousness as long as he or she lives. Like any such highly charged experience it seems to set up a kind of reservoir of strong emotions which can be tapped later with varying degrees of deliberateness and sometimes without any deliberate intention of doing so. But such a sudden and dramatic breakthrough also has certain dangers. Here we shall mention only the danger of mistaking the event for the state—and consequently doing nothing to sustain, nourish and deepen the state of being baptised in the Spirit. As a result it may gradually weaken and eventually disappear.

The delayed-action pattern of entry into the state of being baptised in the Spirit is very frequent, as one can discover by listening to people give witness at charismatic prayer-meetings. The person is prayed over but nothing seems to happen. Then some hours or days later the person finds that the breakthrough has occurred—not convulsively but almost as though the new peace, freedom, power of prayer and so on had slipped into consciousness without being noticed. Once they are adverted to, they begin to blossom further. From a psychological point of view we might perhaps explain this pattern by noting that our spontaneous consciousness tends to set up a resistance when one pushes too hard. Later on, when the pressure is relaxed, the desired effect often occurs. (Anybody who has tried very hard to recall a forgotten name or event will be familiar with this kind of effect in a minor way.) The fact that a baptism in the Spirit which occurs in this pattern is accepted as authentic by the people of the Charismatic Renewal indicates that they realise that what really counts is the *state* of being baptised in the Spirit—even though there is a lot of witness to it as an *event*.

People in the Pentecostal tradition give little prominence, at least in public witness or in writings, to a third way of entry into the state of being baptised in the Spirit—the way I would call the cumulative pattern. This involves a succession of significant religious developments. They occur over a period of perhaps months, often over-lapping each other and interacting in a way that may not be recognised until later. For instance there may be a growing desire for prayer, an apparently unrelated break-through in one's openness to other people, and a healing of old emotional hurts which at first has no obvious connection with the other developments. But each of these contributes to a new and deeper integration of the person. This opens up new areas of spiritual growth. It is perhaps only when the process is well advanced that the person can look back and see something of the overall pattern. Then it becomes clear that the various develop-ments have converged and built up in a way that has brought the person to a state that can accurately be called baptism in the Spirit, and should be recognised as such—even if the person uses some other name, or none at all.

No doubt the gradual process involved in what we have called the cumulative pattern may extend over years in some cases. The more gradual and steady the process, the more difficult it is to recognise it as a process or breakthrough distinct from the Christian life itself. But this does not mean that baptism in the Spirit is less authentic in such cases. For, as we have seen, to be baptised in the Spirit is primarily to have entered into a particular state of consciousness rather than to have undergone some par-ticular kind of event or process.

Conclusion

To pray to be baptised in the Spirit (in its proper sense) is not to look for some esoteric experience. It is simply to pray for an integration of mind and heart in which Christian faith permeates the whole personality, including one's spontaneous feelings and attitudes. One could pray for it in the words of Patrick Kavanagh:

> Feed the gaping need of my senses, and give me ad lib
> To pray unselfconsciously with overflowing speech . . .[5]

And the person whose prayer has been answered, who has been given this gift, can once again borrow lines from Kavanagh to express the result:

> Tranquillity walks with me
> And no care
> O, the quiet ecstasy
> Like a prayer.
>
> I find a star-lovely art
> In a dark sod
> Joy that is timeless! O heart
> That knows God![6]

4. BAPTISM IN THE SPIRIT: THE PENTECOSTAL HERITAGE

I. UNRESOLVED TENSION

The Charismatic Renewal emphasises religion as an *experienced* reality. Having experienced the love and power of God at work in their own hearts and lives, the people of the Renewal want to speak to themselves and others about this tangible work of the Spirit. To do so they need a language—that is, a coherent set of ideas and terms which they can use to articulate their experience. Unfortunately the theology of grace dominant in Catholicism between Trent and Vatican II tended to put grace in an area beyond our conscious experience; and this kind of language was quite unsuitable as an instrument for expressing the charismatic spirituality.

It is not surprising then that even very loyal Catholics involved in this Renewal find they have to use the language of classical Pentecostalism to express some of their most significant religious experiences. This borrowed idiom carries over with it a good deal of what has been called cultural-theological 'baggage',[1] that is, trappings and attitudes which characterise Pentecostalism because of its origin and history. For instance, classical Pentecostalism is rather fundamentalist in its approach to the Bible. It is often naïve in its understanding of God, the world and the problem of evil. And it has an anti-sacramental bias derived from its roots in a very 'low Church' form of Protestantism. So at times it is only with considerable difficulty that Catholics can use this Pentecostal language to express their own spiritual experience. This awkwardness is evident at times in the way they speak about baptism in the Spirit.

Baptism in the Spirit

Anybody who is in contact with the Renewal will be aware

that baptism in the Spirit plays a central role in its spirituality. It is clear that it was an experience of crucial importance in the spiritual development of the leaders of the movement. It figures prominently in the literature. The 'life in the Spirit seminars', designed as an initiation for newcomers, are built around it. In practice, then, one's reaction to baptism in the Spirit often determines one's reaction to the whole movement. But I do not think that the Renewal has as yet fully succeeded either in its theory or in its practice in reconciling the Pentecostal spirituality centred on baptism in the Spirit with traditional Catholic spirituality. So long as this unresolved tension remains, the Charismatic Renewal will not seem fully at home within the mainstream of Catholic life.

The issue is important, even urgent. For this renewal movement has a great deal to contribute to the Church. It has been suggested that the best thing that could happen to the movement would be that it permeate the mainstream of Church life with its charismatic spirituality—and lose its own distinct identity in the process, in much the same way as the liturgical movement did.[2] But there is a major difficulty. The movement has acquired a certain sect-like aura or image. Various things contribute to this —including the emphasis on the gifts of healing, prophecy and tongues. But the usual understanding and presentation of baptism in the Spirit contributes even more, in my opinion, to the impression of a sect. A sect can be distinguished theologically by the fact that its membership consists of those who claim to be 'saved'. The Charismatic Renewal does not limit itself in this way; nor does it identify being 'saved' with being baptised in the Spirit. Theologically, then, it is not a sect. But, looking at it from a sociological point of view, one can see how it could acquire something of the image of a sect despite its best efforts to be universal in its appeal. For it tends to classify people into two groups. Those who claim to have been baptised in the Spirit are, by and large, the 'in' group; while other interested people seem to be on the fringes, or even second-class citizens in the movement. I hasten to add that the leadership of the movement generally takes great pains to avoid this kind of division. But they feel they must emphasise the importance of being baptised in the Spirit. And the almost inevitable by-product of this is the impression that the Renewal is run by a group who think themselves 'a cut above the ordinary Christian'.

It seems, then, that the Renewal finds itself in something of a dilemma. If it emphasises baptism in the Spirit it contributes to the impression that it is sect-like. But if it plays down baptism in the Spirit it may feel that it is abandoning much of the contribution it has to make to the Church. This dilemma may be of real help, if it compels the leadership of the Renewal to look very closely at what is involved in being baptised in the Spirit. It may emerge that what is really basic and of universal significance can be distinguished from the particular shape given to it because of its historical background.

In the last chapter I attempted to provide a basis for this distinction, by outlining what I think is the universally significant core of baptism in the Spirit. The main points of that chapter may be summed up as follows:

1. What is primarily in question in baptism in the Spirit is not an *event* but a *state*.

2. This state can be described simply as having a 'new heart'. It means that a sense of God's redeeming love has transformed the person's spontaneous sentiments, reactions and hopes.

3. This is not an optional extra; rather it ought to be part of normal Christian living.

4. It can begin either suddenly or gradually.

5. People can be distracted from the central 'intrinsic' meaning of baptism in the Spirit by an 'imposed' meaning based on a particular spirituality or theology.

I would like now to look at the particular shape given to baptism in the Spirit in Pentecostalism and in the Charismatic Renewal. In particular I would like to focus on the issue of *suddenness*. I shall try to show why a sudden breakthrough is taken to be the norm. Then I shall consider the problems which this poses for the Charismatic Renewal within the Churches. Finally I shall make some suggestions for easing these problems. In this way I would hope to contribute towards an integration of Pentecostal spirituality with traditional Catholic and Protestant spirituality.

II. HISTORICAL BACKGROUND TO EMPHASIS ON SUDDENNESS

In order to understand why the Pentecostal-Charismatic spirituality lays so much stress on baptism in the Spirit as a sudden event we must look at the tradition of Evangelical Protestantism out of which Pentecostalism came. Of particular interest in this connection is the Evangelical notion of conversion.

At the time of the Reformation the normal Christian would have been baptised as an infant and brought up as a Christian. Conscious initiation into the Christian life would have extended over the whole childhood and adolescence of such a person. First Confession and Communion and the sacrament of Confirmation would then be sacramental high-points in a long and gradual process. These and other public celebrations would be special occasions for the personal appropriation of faith, over and above the normal occasions of personal and community prayer. We certainly cannot presume that Christians generally failed to commit themselves personally to God and to experience his action in their lives. But in this Christian world there would have been a lot of purely nominal Christianity. The Protestant Reformers were convinced that many people had no deep personal experience of the saving grace of Christ and of the work of the Spirit. They felt that some aspects of current Church teaching on grace and sacramental efficacy were a distortion of the Good News of Jesus Christ. One of the great slogans of the Reformation became 'Salvation by grace alone, through faith alone rather than through good works.'

Conversion

Properly understood, this formula is not only sound teaching but is at the heart of the Christian message; it is precisely what St Paul preached. But the Evangelicals, especially in the English-speaking world, more or less gained a monopoly on the formula, 'salvation by grace, through faith'. For them it represented a rejection of Catholic sacramental teaching. The Evangelicals had two objections to the Catholic doctrine on baptism, especially infant baptism. Firstly, they thought it eliminated the need for personal repentance and faith. Secondly, they felt it gave some intrinsic power to the rite of baptism itself—to such an extent that the person was being saved not 'by grace alone' but by this purely human ceremony or 'work'. Evangelical Protestants insisted that one became a Christian not by any sacrament—least of all by infant baptism—but by 'conversion'—that is, by a conscious and deliberate act of turning to God under the influence of his saving grace; or perhaps more accurately, by being turned to God by his grace.

Because of their emphasis on conversion the Evangelicals looked for some definite and even dramatic moment of conscious conversion in *adult* life—such a moment as occurred in the lives of Paul, Augustine, Luther, Wesley and a host of other Protestant 'models'. The suddenness of this type of conversion was taken as proof that this was salvation not by any human effort but by the direct intervention of God.

In the Catholic tradition, on the other hand, what was envisaged was a life-long process in which God acts on and in us, and we respond and grow in grace day by day. This process was understood to begin at infant baptism. The term 'convert' was applied by Catholics to somebody who enters the Church for the first time as an adult; it could also be applied to a repentant sinner. The idea that every Christian had to have a conscious conversion-experience found little place in the Catholic theology of Counter-Reformation times.

Convergence

In recent years there has been a remarkable convergence of the Catholic and Evangelical traditions. Psychological studies showed that what appeared to be a sudden and utterly unexpected conversion, explicable only as an intervention of God, could in fact find a more human explanation: the sudden conscious conversion could be the resolution of a long conflict which had taken place at a subconscious level; and this could also account for the sense of peace and freedom. At first hostile to such 'explanations' of conversion, Evangelicals gradually have come to accept that suddenness is not a necessary and convincing indication that a conversion is 'of grace alone'. And so the possibility of a more

C

gradual and less memorable conversion has become acceptable to most Evangelicals.

Meanwhile Catholic theologians came to appreciate the importance of a 'fundamental option', of an explicit or implicit kind. This meant that the Christian has to make some basic decision for God, a deliberate acceptance of the gift of salvation. In effect this coincided with the more modern Evangelical understanding of conversion.

A major source of disagreement between the two traditions used to be their teaching on the effects of infant baptism. Catholics insisted that the baptised child was a real Christian. Evangelicals saw the rite as a 'mere sign'; for them, real Christianity began with personal conversion. On this issue also there has been considerable convergence of the two traditions. Evangelicals are now less individualistic than before in their understanding of Christian faith. So they are now more inclined to recognise that infant baptism may have a role in bringing the child to share in the life and faith of the Christian community. Meanwhile Catholics have come to appreciate the difference between infant baptism and adult baptism. The new Catholic rite of infant baptism brings out the fact that the child now received into the community of faith will later have to make a personal commitment in faith—when he or she is old enough to respond consciously to God. So it is clear that infant baptism does not operate in some magical way which would relieve the individual of the need to turn personally to God; and this is the crucial point in the Evangelical spirituality, the reason behind their insistence on conversion.

An important difference between the two traditions used to be in their different attitudes to the experience of grace. The Evangelicals presupposed that the saving work of God was a matter of experience. Indeed 'assurance' of the presence of grace became a matter of major importance for many of them; and 'inward feeling' was often seen as a test of the reality of conversion. In post-Tridentine Catholicism the rigid distinction between nature and grace led people to think that there could be no direct knowledge or experience of grace; and 'mere' feelings were very much distrusted.

On this issue also there is a convergence of the two traditions.

Nowadays most Evangelicals, and the more moderate Pentecostalists, are well aware of the dangers of an excessive appeal to or dependence on the emotions. And two important changes have taken place in Catholic thinking on the issue. Firstly, it is now widely accepted that it was a mistake to locate supernatural grace in a realm quite beyond experience. Secondly, a more integrated view of human consciousness enables Catholics to realise that religious feelings are not 'mere' sense experiences but may be responses of the whole person—and at the same time movements of grace in the heart of the Christian.

What emerges from all this is that when misunderstandings are removed and when each tradition has taken what is true and valuable in the other, the remaining differences are minor. Indeed it turns out that even in the past the major differences between the two traditions had less to do with the *theology* of how a person is turned to God than with its *psychology*—the Evangelicals giving a privileged place to a sudden breakthrough while the Catholics emphasised a life-long process.

A second blessing

The stress in Pentecostalism on baptism in the Spirit as a sudden and decisive breakthrough can be traced back to the Evangelical tradition out of which it sprang. Pentecostalism has its origin in this tradition, at a time before it had begun to converge again with the Catholic tradition.

Within Evangelical Protestantism there were various groups who laid special stress on holiness. In the English-speaking world most of these groups were Methodist or were influenced by the Methodist teaching on sanctification and perfection. The founder of Methodism, John Wesley, had always been interested in holiness. He developed and adapted those elements of Protestant tradition which supplemented 'justification' (which was understood by Protestants to be an extrinsic and legal affair) with 'regeneration' (a re-birth to a new nature) and 'sanctification'. At the time of his conversion Wesley expected to receive not only justification and regeneration but total sanctification as well. But experience taught him that total sanctity does not come in the moment of conversion. Some years later a number of

Wesley's converts claimed to have had a *second* dramatic intervention by God, this time bringing the total eradication of sin from the heart. So Wesley developed his doctrine of 'perfection' or 'entire sanctification'. He held that every converted Christian should look forward to such a 'second blessing', an experience rather similar to conversion, and also brought about by grace, through faith.[3]

After Wesley's time, some strands in the Methodist movement continued to stress the importance of this second blessing, bringing the gift of entire sanctification. These, along with some other strands in the Evangelical tradition, played a major part in the 'holiness movements' which were a feature of nineteenth-century English-speaking Protestantism.[4] The second blessing which they preached was sometimes referred to as a baptism in the Spirit.

Pentecostalism

The step from there to the Pentecostal view of baptism in the Spirit is a short but significant one. It was a matter of a shift of emphasis in the second blessing from personal sanctification to the charismatic gifts of the Spirit and an 'empowering' for witness to others. This step was taken at about the turn of this century by some fundamentalist Protestants in America; and that was the beginning of Pentecostalism. Taking the first Pentecost as their model, they held that baptism in the Spirit is a second blessing (i.e. it is given some time after the first 'blessing', which is conversion); in it the power of the Spirit is poured out; this is shown in various charismatic gifts; and the one sure and indispensable sign of the authenticity of the experience is the gift of tongues.

The Pentecostalists quoted Scripture texts in support of their position. But their reading of the Bible was mistaken. They were quite correct in seeing in the Bible an insistence on conscious experience of the work of the Spirit in the heart and life of the true Christian. But they failed to realise that in the New Testament this is not reserved for those who have had a second conversion-experience. Rather the assumption of the early Church was that *every* Christian is 'baptised' or 'anointed' with the Spirit.[5]

Having been squeezed out of their own Churches, the Pentecostalists formed their own Churches—often called 'Assemblies'.
These and their off-shoots are now flourishing in every continent.
Their prophetic-type leadership and structure, their long and
enthusiastic prayer-services, their healing ministries, their fundamentalism, their stress on the role of spirits, their community
spirit, all make them especially attractive in Africa and Latin
America. They appeal particularly to people who are on the
margins of the emergent urban society in the Third World, since
they offer a certain security and promise answers to many of
their religious and secular needs.

The Charismatic Renewal

For many years the Catholic Church and the main Protestant
Churches were strongly opposed to any form of Pentecostalism.
But recently a remarkable change has taken place. A Pentecostal
spirituality has emerged within these Churches. The movement
is sometimes called 'neo-Pentecostalism'. But a more common
name is 'the Charismatic Movement'. Those who are involved
often insist that it is not really a movement; the name they
prefer to use is 'the Charismatic Renewal'. A number of people
feel that the words 'charismatic' and 'renewal' should not become
the monopoly of any one group. This is a valid point. But we
can accept the title 'Charismatic Renewal' as a name, while continuing to use the individual words in a wider sense when that is
appropriate. The aim of the Renewal is to transform the Churches
from within by emphasising the charismatic gifts of the Holy
Spirit and the conscious experience of the love, peace and joy of
life in Christ. It sees baptism in the Spirit as the decisive breakthrough which opens a person to receive these personal and
'ministerial' gifts.

Catholics involved in the Charismatic Renewal have been
working hard to integrate elements of the Pentecostal spirituality
into the Catholic tradition. One major point on which they have
adapted Pentecostal theology is that they present baptism in the
Spirit as the release of the Spirit or of the power and gifts of the
Spirit, that is, an activation of what has already been given in
(infant) baptism. Furthermore, they do not insist that 'tongues'

is the sure and indispensable test of a genuine baptism in the Spirit. But they generally hold that this gift ought to be normal for anybody who has been baptised in the Spirit.

Despite the efforts of the theologians associated with the Charismatic Renewal, there remains, as we noted earlier, a certain unresolved tension in the spirituality of the movement between the Pentecostal and the Catholic heritages. Hopefully the brief historical account we have just given will indicate why this tension exists. Basically it stems from the fact that Pentecostalism has its roots in an old-fashioned Evangelical Protestantism—and it takes its preconceptions from that source. So it puts a very high value on a sudden and dramatic breakthrough, because it sees in this suddenness an indication of the hand of God. For Pentecostalists, as for the Evangelicals of the past (and some today), a sudden breakthrough is a 'proof' that the person is being saved 'by grace alone'.

III. A LEGACY OF PENTECOSTALISM

The Charismatic Renewal in the main Christian Churches has inherited from Pentecostalism a particular model of the form in which baptism in the Spirit should come about. This is the one I have called 'the dramatic pattern' (see the end of the last chapter). Many people involved in the Renewal have had just such a dramatic breakthrough, while they were being prayed over. Obviously, such people have no personal reason to question this model.

Many others now associated with the Renewal have received baptism in the Spirit in the form which I have called 'the delayed-action pattern'. They remained unmoved while they were being prayed over; but the desired change stole in on them some hours, or perhaps days, later. Though they do not quite fit the ideal model, their experience is so common, and the change is so remarkable in its own way, that this form of baptism in the Spirit is acknowledged in the Renewal as fully authentic; and people often mention it in giving witness to others.

Some people in the Renewal have been baptised in the Spirit in the form I have called 'the cumulative pattern'. So they cannot give any precise date when they experienced baptism in the

Spirit as an *event*. But they recall that over a certain period of time (some days or weeks or months) they came to experience the same effects as those who had a more sudden and dramatic experience. Aware of the gift of God's love and peace, they are not troubled by nagging doubts about the authenticity of their baptism in the Spirit. They don't hanker for a single dramatic happening. The fact that the generally accepted idiom of Pentecostalism refers to baptism in the Spirit as a sudden breakthrough doesn't disturb them. They are sufficiently secure and independent to follow the Spirit in the way he leads them, even when this does not fit the accepted pattern.

However, there are others involved in the Renewal, or on its fringes, who are troubled by the Pentecostal ideal of baptism in the Spirit. Some decide that they do not want such a dramatic and emotional experience; others conclude that they are incapable of it. This may cause some to abandon the whole shared-prayer movement. Others continue to attend the prayer-meetings but feel themselves to be second-class citizens—and this feeling is reinforced every time they hear anybody giving witness to having been baptised in the Spirit.

There are people whose temperament is not congenial to dramatic religious experiences; but some of these people may hanker after such a dramatic breakthrough; and they may be encouraged to do so by the way in which baptism in the Spirit is presented in the Renewal. The result may be a serious hampering of their religious development. Some of them may become discouraged by their repeated failure to attain the breakthrough they are seeking. Others may build up so much psychological pressure that they eventually do have a dramatic breakthrough—but it may be unduly explosive, or harmful in some other way.

These difficulties are a direct result of the acceptance by the Renewal of a particular model of baptism in the Spirit as *the* way in which the gift of a 'new heart' is given by God to the Christian. I must add at once that not everybody in the Renewal holds this view. But it is the dominant and approved viewpoint. So long as this great stress on suddenness remains, no amount of personal sympathy with people who do not fit the pattern will eliminate the problems. There will be pressure to fit the pattern—and this, perhaps more than anything else, will give the Renewal the image and the attitude of a sect. The Charismatic Renewal cannot be universal in its appeal until it recognises that there is a variety of ways in which a Christian can come to experience the faith in a truly living manner. It must be accepted that to be baptised in the Spirit is primarily a state rather than an event. And the state can be present in somebody who has had no single dramatic experience which could be labelled baptism in the Spirit as an event.[6]

Some of the people who are so anxious to be baptised in the Spirit in the dramatic form, may be prevented by their anxiety from attaining the state in a more gradual manner. Indeed some who had already been in that state, at least in some degree, may have had it weakened or destroyed by becoming convinced that they have not yet had the dramatic breakthrough. It is tragic that such people are made to feel spiritually inadequate because an unduly limited conception of baptism in the Spirit is imposed on them.

Correction

That baptism in the Spirit can come about suddenly cannot be denied. That it is permissible to pray for it, to yearn for it, even to be prayed over for it, should not any longer be denied; though there is need for some careful discernment about who, when, where and how this praying ought to be done.[7] But the leaders of the Charismatic Renewal ought to recognise that the Pentecostal heritage needs to be corrected in relation to suddenness (as they have already corrected it on other points).

This process of correction ought to take place at different levels. In the local prayer-groups there is need for a new kind of testimony, given this time by people whose entry into the state of baptism in the Spirit was a gradual and cumulative process. People listening to this kind of witness, given alongside the witness of those who have had a more dramatic breakthrough, would be saved from the pressure to conform to a particular pattern. The emphasis would be where it ought to be—on the power of God to work in any way he chooses, and on the daily living experience of his love—rather than on a single dramatic incident. At one stroke this would rescue the prayer-group from most of the elements of a sect-like image which it might have. It would enable the prayer-group to appeal to people with a wider variety of religious experience. All this could be done without any playing down of the importance of being baptised in the Spirit.

Correction at the purely local level is not enough. The international leadership of the Charismatic Renewal should be widened so that it can be clearly seen to represent a broader spectrum of religious experience than it seems to at present.

The publishing agencies which cater for the religious reading appetite of people of the Renewal ought, I think, to make available a good deal of writing based on the experience of people whose religious development followed a cumulative rather than a dramatic pattern. This new stream of literature would complement rather than replace the kind of writing that is currently in circulation.

The official or semi-official publications also require correction on some points. In particular, the manual of the 'Life in the Spirit' seminars—a book which has enormous influence in shaping the religious experience of the people of the Renewal—requires modification.[8] It ought to be adapted so that it no longer appears to 'canonise' a sudden breakthrough as the norm. The 'Life in the Spirit' seminars themselves can be very valuable. For many people they are a far more effective form of religious education than any instruction they have heard or courses they have followed. So I see no reason why they should be abandoned or their importance minimised. But I do think there ought to be less of a psychological build-up for the ceremony of being prayed over. No matter how delicately this is handled, the present pattern of the seminars leads to considerable pressure on participants to conform to a Pentecostal-type model of baptism in the Spirit.

Corrections of the kind I am suggesting are in line with developments which have been taking place within the Renewal fairly recently. For example there is now more stress than previously on the religious development of Christians *after* they have been baptised in the Spirit. This is just one instance of elements of a more typically Catholic type of spirituality being brought in to replace or supplement aspects of the Pentecostal spirituality which have been found somewhat inadequate. So I would hope that the points I am making about the need for some modifications would not be seen as a threat but rather as an invitation to move boldly forward along lines already implicit in the Renewal.

It is very important that the Charismatic Renewal should experience and foster an ever greater convergence of what is best in the Pentecostal, Protestant and Catholic outlooks. This will widen the spirituality of the Renewal to a point where it can become co-terminous with the spirituality of Christianity itself. This will be a type of practical and lived ecumenism which will be of great benefit to the Church. One of the best illustrations of this point is to be found in the conception of baptism in the Spirit which has been our concern in this and the previous chapter. It is a borrowing from Pentecostalism which, when purged of its 'cultural baggage', can be of great benefit to Catholics and Protestants.

The witness to baptism in the Spirit given by people of the Charismatic Renewal can be a help to various categories of Christians:

—It *articulates* for many fervent Christians an aspect of their religious experience which did not find adequate recognition in the more common Catholic and Protestant spiritualities.

—It is a real *challenge* to those who have been drifting along in a half-hearted commitment to Christianity; it invites them to take their faith more seriously.

—It gives *hope* to many Christians who have been struggling along, feeling oppressed by worry or fears, enslaved to bad habits, hampered by scruples, plagued by insecurity, or deadened by selfishness; it encourages such people to look forward to a real and experienced spiritual liberation. Inspired by the witness of others who were rescued from a similar plight, they begin to pray with confidence for such a liberation. They also begin to take other practical steps which might hasten the time of liberation. One such step is to be prayed over by others. The circumstances in which this should be encouraged is an interesting and important question. It is however too large an issue to take up here. So I shall return to it in chapter 8.

PART THREE

NAMING THE EXPERIENCE

5. WHAT'S IN A NAME?

In chapter 3 I tried to discern what is the central core of the religious experience called baptism in the Spirit. I suggested that it is primarily the state of having a 'new heart'; and I pointed out that this state can come about in a variety of ways or patterns. In chapter 4 I went on to show why just one of these patterns, the dramatic one, has come to have a monopoly of the term 'baptism in the Spirit'; and I suggested that the imbalance ought to be corrected. In this chapter I would like to look more closely at the term itself. So I shall examine the biblical connotations of the phrase to see whether, or in what sense, there is any basis in the Bible for the use of the term in the sense in which it is used by Pentecostalists or 'charismatics'—or any basis for the somewhat more extended meaning of the term which I have proposed.

A suitable term?

Why use the term 'baptism in the Spirit' at all? Is it not at best confusing, if not positively misleading? Clearly the main reason why this term is applied to the religious experience in question is a historical one—namely, that the Pentecostalists used it to describe what is basically the same experience. They used it because their whole theology centred on the text in which Christ told his apostles to wait in Jerusalem until they were 'baptised with the Holy Spirit' (*Acts* 1 : 5). Pentecost (*Acts* 2 1-4) was seen as the fulfilment of this promise; and the coming of the Holy Spirit on Cornelius and his party (*Acts* 10 : 44) showed that other believers were to have their own Pentecost, that they too were to be baptised with the Holy Spirit.

But the question we are asking now is not this historical one.

Rather it is whether there is any adequate intrinsic reason for the use of the term 'baptism in the Spirit' to describe the kind of experience to which it is applied today. Let us presume that chapter 3 gives a reasonably accurate account of the core of the experience common to Pentecostalists and 'charismatics' today. The question now is whether one is entitled to call it 'baptism in the Spirit', not simply because Pentecostalists have been using that term but because of some intrinsic elements in the experience itself. I believe that there are good intrinsic reasons for the use of the term; but they are not entirely compelling. The most I would claim is that the term is quite a good one. I prefer it to other possible terms. But that is mostly because it is already in possession.[1] It is true that the term creates certain difficulties because it has acquired some unacceptable connotations from its Pentecostal background; for instance in its present usage it is more likely to refer to a sudden event than to an enduring state. But it seems to me that it is more important from a theological and ecumenical point of view to accept the term and try to rescue it from misleading connotations than to coin a new term, or to import from the Eastern Church some term that is scarcely known in the West,[2] or to leave the experience without a name.

The word 'baptism'

To provide a background against which we can judge the suitability of the term 'baptism in the Spirit' we shall first examine the meaning of the word 'baptism'[3] and then go on to see if there is any point in adding the phrase 'in the Spirit'.

Outside Jewish and Christian circles the normal meaning of the Greek verb 'baptizō' was a secular one—to saturate or soak or immerse or inundate. In late Old Testament and early Christian times it was occasionally used in a more religious sense, especially in the mystery cults of the time where it sometimes signified purification and sometimes suggested the conferring of new life.

It was only in late Old Testament times that the word came into widespread use in Jewish circles. For the Jews it normally referred to the ceremonial washings performed frequently for the removal of ritual uncleanness; there is no evidence of a direct

borrowing of the idea of purification from the mystery cults—
and no need to postulate it since the notion of washing easily
suggests the idea of purification. At about the time of Christ the
word 'baptizō' came to have a more specialised meaning for
the Jews; it came to refer to a ritual washing which was part
of the reception rite for converts to Judaism. The significant
point is that the word had now got a once-for-all implication; it
involved entry into a new way of life.

Baptism in the New Testament

The baptisms carried out by John the Baptist can be seen as
a further development along these lines. For the Baptist, the rite
had a 'once only' character and implied the beginning of a new
kind of life. But there were important differences. John's stress
was not on ritual purity but on real moral conversion. His was
'a baptism of repentance for the forgiveness of sins' (*Mark* 1:4).
It involved strict moral obligations: 'Bear fruit that befits
repentance' (*Matt.* 3:8). 'Rob no one by violence or by false
accusation, and be content with your wages' (*Luke* 3:14). Perhaps even more importantly, John's baptism had a very strong
escatological dimension: it looked forward to the Messianic Age.
He insisted that it had meaning only as a preparation for the
imminent coming of the Lord in judgment (*Matt.* 3:11-12).

With the accounts of the baptism of Jesus the word 'baptism'
takes on richer and deeper connotations. Mark's account presents
the event as the occasion for a remarkable religious experience
of Jesus himself—a new and special consciousness of his divine
sonship: 'And when he came up out of the water, immediately
he saw the heavens opened and the Spirit descending on him
like a dove; and a voice came from heaven, "Thou art my beloved
son; with thee I am well pleased."' (*Mark* 1:10-11). This
passage is strongly reminiscent of the first 'Servant Song' in
Isaiah:

Behold my servant, whom I uphold,
my chosen, in whom my soul delights;
I have put my Spirit upon him,
he will bring forth justice to the nations. (*Is.* 42:1).

So there is the suggestion that Jesus experienced not merely a vivid awareness of being cherished as the Son but also a strong sense of mission—of being called to bring God's justice to the world and hope to the oppressed, as the later verses of the Isaian passage make clear:

> I have called you ... taken you by the hand ...
> I have given you as a covenant to the people
> a light to the nations,
> to open the eyes that are blind,
> to bring out the prisoners from the dungeon ... (*Is.* 42 : 6-7).

So the baptism of Jesus is seen as the inauguration of the Kingdom. In this context the references to the outpouring of the Spirit are particularly significant. At his baptism Jesus is *empowered* by the Spirit and at once he begins to be *led* by the Spirit: '. . . Jesus full of the Spirit returned from the Jordan and was led by the Spirit . . .' (*Luke* 4 : 1) 'And Jesus returned in the power of the Spirit into Galilee . . .' (*Luke* 4 : 14). His sense of mission leads Jesus to look forward to his death: 'I have a baptism to be baptised with; and how I am constrained until it is accomplished.' (*Luke* 12 : 49). He will be 'baptised' (immersed) in suffering in order to purify the earth (the 'fire' of the previous verse) and inaugurate the New Age.

Against this background of what baptism means for Jesus we can see the significance of the relatively few references in the New Testament to the baptism of his followers. Already in Peter's first great sermon after Pentecost we find the most important points. Baptism is in the *name of Jesus Christ*; it is a baptism of *repentance* for the *forgiveness of sin*; it is associated with the *gift of the Holy Spirit,* in fulfilment of the *promise* of the Messianic Age, to which *all are called.* (*Acts* 2 : 38-9; cf. 10 : 47; 22 : 16.)

Baptism is a proclamation of faith and a formal, symbolic expression of it. The person who believes in Jesus goes on to be baptised in his name—e.g. ' "Believe in the Lord Jesus and you will be saved" . . . and he was baptised at once.' (*Acts* 16 : 31-3; cf. 8 : 36; 9 : 18; 16 : 15; 18 : 8).

The mission mandate at the end of the Synoptic Gospels shows that baptism is seen as the formal entry rite into the community of believers: 'Go . . . make disciples of all nations, baptising them in the name of the Father and of the Son and of the Holy Spirit . . . and lo, I am with you . . .' (*Matt.* 28:19). 'He who believes and is baptised will be saved . . .' (*Mark* 16:16). And the parallel text in Luke stresses the importance of the promised Holy Spirit who will clothe the followers of Jesus 'with power from on high' (*Luke* 24:49).

In St Paul, the key text about baptism is Romans 6:3-11: we have been baptised into Christ, which means that we share in his death and in his resurrection; so for the future we can live the life of Christ. Paul here brings out the symbolism of the rite itself—going down into the water and coming up again; and at the same time he insists on its real effect in us. A corresponding text in Colossians (2:12-14) brings out the fact that it is 'through *faith* in the working of God' that this takes place. And in Galatians (3:27-9), Paul insists that to be baptised into Christ means that Christians join a community where 'there is neither Jew nor Greek, . . . slave nor free, . . . male nor female; for all are one in Christ Jesus.' This theme of the unity of the baptised community is very important for Paul. He insists on the *moral implications* of having 'one body, one Spirit, one hope, one Lord, one faith, one baptism, one God and Father of us all' (*Eph.* 4:4-6). If Christians are 'all baptised into one body . . . and all . . . made to drink of one Spirit', then they must work together in mutual respect and support. Since all have been washed and sanctified in baptism (*Eph.* 5:26; I *Cor.* 6:11), then there is no room for factionalism (I *Cor.* 1:13-16).

An appropriate word?

This survey of the meaning of the term 'baptism' leaves us in a position to ask whether it is an appropriate word to designate what people mean when they say they have been baptised in the Spirit. The first thing to note is the extraordinary richness of meaning which the term 'baptism' has in the New Testament. To list the different shades of meaning is to end up with something so all-embracing that it could be taken as a description of all that is distinctive in a full, conscious, living out of the Christian faith. It is precisely this comprehensiveness which makes the word 'baptism' especially apt when applied to the kind of religious awakening and the state of Christian awareness which is the core of being 'baptised in the Spirit'.

In order to bring out this comprehensiveness let us briefly summarise the connotations of the word 'baptism'. Here we put together the aspects which are central in the baptism of Jesus, with those which are specifically mentioned in regard to his followers; for the text from Romans (6: 3-11) shows that to be baptised into Christ is to share *his* life, and therefore his sense of the Fatherhood of God, of being led by the Spirit and of being sent to the world. As we list the various items, it can be noted that each of them seems to be an accurate description of some element in the religious experience called 'baptism in the Spirit'. Baptism in the New Testament involves:

—entry into a new kind of life;
—the breaking of the power of sin;
—faith in, and surrender to, Christ as Lord;
—a share in Christ's sense of sonship of the Father;
—a sense of being filled with the Spirit and empowered by him;
—a sense of mission, of being sent to share the Good News with others;
—the experience of being guided by the Spirit;
—an awareness of belonging to the community of believers in Christ.

Underpinning all these aspects of meaning in the word 'baptism' lies its literal meaning as 'saturation' or 'immersion'. For to be baptised, in its New Testament sense, is to be immersed in Christ, to have one's conscious life saturated with the awareness that one is living his life. Perhaps more than any other aspect of the meaning of the word 'baptism' it is this literal meaning which makes it particularly appropriate to convey what is involved in the experience called 'baptism in the Spirit'. For the fundamental element in that experience is a kind of 'soaking' in the loving mercy of God; the person's consciousness is immersed in an awareness of the nearness and unconditional love of God.

Because of this literal meaning underpinning the more specifically religious meanings, the word 'baptism' in its biblical sense retains a certain ambivalence which enables it to refer both to an enduring state and to the event which initiates that state. The reference to the event of baptism is more obvious, of course. But the event is significant only in so far as it is the beginning of the state of being baptised. This is a pretty exact parallel to what is involved in baptism in the Spirit. In chapter 3 I suggested that this has two shades of meaning: it can refer to an event or to a state; and of the two the state is more important, though the event may be more obvious. Here we have the basis for an answer to the major argument against the use of the term 'baptism in the Spirit', the argument that it is too confusing, since the word 'baptism' in common usage refers to the sacrament of baptism. But before considering that argument in detail we must first look at the phrase 'in the Spirit' and see what significance it can have.

'In the Spirit'

The Pentecostalists make a rather facile distinction between 'mere water baptism' and 'baptism in the Spirit'. The present use of the phrase 'baptism in the Spirit' in the Charismatic Renewal derives historically from this distinction. But the Pentecostalist 'playing down' of sacramental baptism is not generally accepted in the Charismatic Renewal, at least in Catholic circles. Where then does that leave the last three words of the term 'baptism in the Spirit'? Is there any particular reason for referring to the Spirit at all, or is it just a hang-over from Pentecostalism? The best way to answer these questions is to look closely at some passages in the New Testament, passages that tell us what it meant to live fully as a Christian in New Testament times. We shall find that references to the Holy Spirit are very frequent in such passages, especially in the Pauline epistles. In fact it is easy to find texts in which Paul *attributes to the Holy Spirit* precisely those features which we noted as characteristic of the religious experience called 'baptism in the Spirit' and which we also noted as part of the connotation of the word 'baptism' in its biblical setting.

First of all there is the sense of being accepted as the cherished child of God to such an extent that God can be addressed as 'dearest Father' ('Abba'). Paul attributes this to the Holy Spirit: 'God has sent the Spirit of his Son into our hearts, crying

"Abba, Father!" ' (*Gal.* 4:6). 'When we cry, "Abba, Father!" it is the Spirit himself bearing witness with our spirit that we are children of God.' (*Rom.* 8:15-16).

Christians are aware that they have become capable of loving in a way that is beyond their own powers and seems to be a share in God's own love. St Paul attributes this to the Spirit: 'God's love has been poured into our hearts through the Holy Spirit which has been given to us' (*Rom.* 5:5). And to the Spirit too is attributed the sense of being set free from fear (*Rom.* 8:15) and from sin and death (*Rom.* 8:2). The Christian has the experience of being led by the Spirit in daily living (*Gal.* 5:16, 25).

These descriptions of aspects of what it meant to be a Christian in New Testament times parallel closely the account given by people nowadays who try to describe the effect of being 'baptised in the Spirit'. Such people also speak of the hope they experience, in words that echo the prayer of Paul for the Romans: '. . . that by the power of the Holy Spirit you may abound in hope' (*Rom.* 15:13). Paul prays for the Ephesians that the Father will grant them 'to be strengthened with might through his Spirit in the inner man' (*Eph.* 3:16); and this sense of inner strength is likewise witnessed to by people who claim to be baptised in the Spirit. In describing their new enriched experience of Christianity such people could easily borrow this passage from Paul: '. . . the fruit of the Spirit is love, joy, peace, patience, kindness, goodness, faithfulness, gentleness, self-control' (*Gal.* 5:22).

People who speak of being 'baptised in the Spirit' almost invariably testify that their faith has become real and alive. Very frequently this is experienced concretely as a vivid conviction of the Lordship of Jesus—meaning not merely that the divinity of Jesus is acknowledged but that the person is determined to allow Jesus to take over as the Lord of his or her daily life. Paul insists that this kind of faith is the work of the Holy Spirit: '. . . no one can say "Jesus is Lord" except by the Holy Spirit' (1 *Cor.* 12:3).

Testimonies to baptism in the Spirit nearly always lay special emphasis on the gift of prayer; they speak of a burning thirst for prayer, of an ability to pray with quite unexpected intensity and even at times of the sense of some transcendent power praying within the person almost independently of the person's own feelings. Paul attributes such effects to the Holy Spirit: 'Likewise the Spirit helps us in our weakness; for we do not know how to pray as we ought, but the Spirit himself intercedes for us with sighs too deep for words.' (*Rom.* 8:26). '. . . pray at all times in the Spirit' (*Eph.* 6:18).

This gift of prayer, coming from the Spirit, frequently involves the ability to pray freely and joyfully with others: '. . . be filled with the Spirit, addressing one another in psalms and hymns and spiritual songs, singing and making melody to the Lord with all your heart, always and for everything giving thanks in the name of our Lord Jesus Christ to God the Father.' (*Eph.* 6:18-20).

St Paul in his first letter to the Corinthians speaks at some length of the variety of gifts given by the Spirit for the *service* of the Christian community:

> Now there are varieties of gifts, but the same Spirit . . . To each is given the manifestation of the Spirit for the common good. To one is given through the Spirit the utterance of wisdom, and to another the utterance of knowledge according to the same Spirit, to another faith by the same Spirit, to another gifts of healing by the one Spirit, to another the working of miracles, to another prophecy, to another the ability to distinguish between spirits, to another various kinds of tongues. All these are inspired by one and the same Spirit, who apportions to each one individually as he wills.
>
> (1 *Cor.* 12:4-11).

This passage has of course been treated as both a charter and a directory by Pentecostal and 'charismatic' groups. Some would say that such groups mould their religious experience to fit their particular interpretation of Paul's list of charisms. But it can scarcely be denied that the experience of Pentecostalists and 'charismatics' has helped the Church in general to take the whole passage more seriously and not to be so quick to explain away the various gifts as inapplicable to Christian living today.

Old Testament and New Testament meaning

This brief survey of New Testament passages describing the

Christian experience indicates the decisive role played in that experience by the Holy Spirit. It should perhaps be noted here that when the Spirit is spoken of in the New Testament the overtones of meaning are not quite the same as when the Spirit is spoken of in later theology. The reason is that it was only during New Testament times that the distinction between Father, Son and Spirit came to be recognised. Prior to that time the phrase 'the Spirit of God' would have meant some aspect of God, especially in relation to his action on the world and on humans, rather than a distinct person within a Trinity. The references to the Spirit in New Testament writings carry over a good deal of this meaning; in some cases the meaning is far closer to the Old Testament conception than to that of later Christian theology. Consequently, the term 'baptism in the Holy Spirit', understood in a New Testament sense, would not be likely to suggest some exclusive relationship with the Spirit as distinct from the Father or Christ. A more exclusive relationship is suggested only if we think of the Spirit in the more specific terms of later theology. The New Testament sense of the term 'baptism in the Spirit' would include the general idea of being immersed in the life and power of God, as well as a more specific relationship to the Holy Spirit.

Even when we consider the Holy Spirit in his more distinctive, personal role as this emerges in the New Testament we find that he is seen precisely as the Spirit of Christ and the gift of the Father. His presence, his activity, is the way in which Christ and the Father come into the daily living of the Christian. *So, to be 'baptised in the Spirit' means no more and no less than to be baptised as a Christian.*

Only one baptism

From all this we must conclude that the last three words of the term 'baptism in the Spirit' are truly meaningful. They indicate what baptism is all about, bringing out more explicitly a range of meaning that is already contained in some degree in the New Testament understanding of the word 'baptism'. But the words 'in the Spirit' do not distinguish 'baptism in the Spirit' as one particular kind of baptism over against some other kind of baptism which is not 'in the Spirit'. From the New Testament point of view the only other baptism with which it could be contrasted meaningfully is that of John the Baptist; and the Acts of the Apostles leaves us in no doubt that John's baptism has been superseded, so that it is not an option for a Christian (*Acts* 19:1-9). This passage makes it clear that to be baptised in the name of Jesus (v. 5) is the same thing as to be baptised into the Holy Spirit (vv. 2-3).

It must be said then that the New Testament does not support the Pentecostalist theory that baptism in the Spirit is a 'second blessing', distinct from and subsequent to the believer's conversion to Christ and initiation into the Christian community. In a detailed study of the meaning of 'baptism in the Spirit' in the New Testament, James D. G. Dunn documents this conclusion thoroughly. He points out that after the decisive initiation into Christ there can be further experiences of being 'filled' with the Spirit or 'empowered' by him.[4] For instance he refers to Acts 4:31—'And when they had prayed, the place in which they were gathered together was shaken; and they were all filled with the Holy Spirit' and to Acts 13:9—'. . . Paul, filled with the Holy Spirit, looked intently at him . . .' In both these cases it is clear that the people involved had been 'filled with the Spirit' on previous occasions. Dunn insists that the term 'baptism in the Spirit' refers to the original conversion and initiation experience rather than to some such later experience.[5]

In so far as Dunn has shown that the New Testament does not envisage a second blessing in the Pentecostalist sense, I would entirely agree with him. But I think we should see a certain continuity between the first experience of being 'filled with the Spirit' and later instances of the same kind. It is significant that the first of the two texts just quoted seems to be an echo of the account of Pentecost, with its reference to the shaking of the place where they were gathered. Our survey of the meaning of the word 'baptism' suggests that the New Testament does not warrant a sharp disjunction between the event of initiation and the ongoing reality of Christian faith. To be baptised is to be baptised in the Spirit, and it means to be immersed day by day in the life of Christ. So on the basis of the New Testament evidence we come to the same conclusion as we came to in a previous chapter on the basis of a study of religious experience. This conclusion is that baptism in the Spirit as an *event* is significant only in so far as it is the initiation of baptism in the Spirit as an enduring *state*.

6. THE SACRAMENT OF BAPTISM

In the last chapter we found that the New Testament does not support the Pentecostalist conception of baptism in the Spirit as a second blessing, subsequent to Christian conversion and initiation. Should we conclude from this that the whole attempt in the Charismatic Renewal to preserve the fundamental Pentecostalist stress on baptism in the Spirit while correcting certain key points, is a pointless exercise? Quite a number of theologians, sympathetic to the general 'charismatic' trend, and accepting the value of some kind of spiritual awakening in adult life, would nevertheless baulk at the use of the term 'baptism in the Spirit'.[1] They would argue that the New Testament does not sanction any distinction between the sacrament of baptism and 'baptism in the Spirit'. And they would add that in everyday usage the word 'baptism' refers to the sacrament. Why then introduce confusion by defending the use of the phrase 'baptism in the Spirit' in a new and different sense?

This objection can be met head-on by saying that, despite appearances, we are not in fact dealing here with two distinct realities. We are not introducing a new and different meaning for the word baptism but rather drawing out the full connotations and implications of what is involved in the sacrament of baptism. To accept that sacramental baptism is fundamentally different from 'baptism in the Spirit' (in the sense proposed in previous chapters) is to miss the whole point of what the sacrament of baptism really means.

The sacrament of baptism includes a sign aspect and a reality that is signified. What I am suggesting is that the reality signified is not simply the initiation of the Christian into faith and life in Christ, but also the ongoing reality of that faith and life. Christian faith is not something that is given once-for-all in a way that leaves one possessing it independently. It is a continual gift, dependent from moment to moment on the action of the Spirit. One is being continually baptised into Christ in the biblical sense, being immersed in the love and power of God through the Spirit. In order to express the reality of our life in Christ we need to use two different models at the same time. The first is that of a new kind of life given definitively and in some way possessed by the Christian. The second is that of a continually renewed gift freely given to us at each successive instant and never possessed or controlled by us. The rite of baptism signifies our life in Christ and initiates it formally.

The sign aspect

To be quite accurate one should say that it is not merely the rite of baptism but the whole sacramental rite of initiation— which for adults includes confirmation and Eucharist as well as the baptismal rite—which symbolises and formally initiates life in Christ.[2] The fact that the Eucharist is part of this rite of initiation strengthens the case for saying that what is symbolised is not just the entry into the new life but the ongoing reality of it, or the entry into it from moment to moment. Because obviously the Eucharist symbolises and sacramentally effects a state of union with Christ and the Church. However, in order not to confuse the issue I shall concentrate on baptism in what follows.[3]

I have said that the rite of baptism symbolises the continual immersion of the believer in Christ. I would now like to add that there is a real continuity between this primordial sign and a whole range of other symbolic acts performed by the Christian. For instance the renewal of the promises of baptism keep alive the sign aspect of baptism. So too does the use by Catholics of holy water and of the sign of the cross. When Protestants in prayer repeat the solemn formula 'in Jesus' name' they are re-affirming the formula of baptism where the believer is baptised in the name of Christ. So, just as the reality signified by the rite of baptism is an ongoing reality, so too there is a sense in which Christians feel the need to keep the sign renewed and alive. Technically we do not consider that such renewals are sacramental in the strict sense. But they are integral to the life of the

Church and so they share in, and articulate, the sacramental character of the Church itself. For the Church is the primal sacrament which gives meaning to particular sacraments and quasi-sacramental acts.

The reality that is signified

Having noted these points about the sign aspect of baptism it is time to concentrate on the reality that is signified. I am suggesting that this has a two-fold aspect—the entry into the new life and the ongoing immersion in it. In other words the reality signified is both an event and a state. In order to show that the reality signified in a sacrament can have such a two-fold aspect let us think for a moment about two other sacraments. The sacrament of marriage means both the state of being married and the event that began it. This ambiguity is not just an unfortunate accident. Rather it is basic to the nature of the sacrament.[4] In much the same way the phrase 'Eucharistic community' can refer to the Christian community both in its celebration of the Eucharist and in its everyday Christian living; again the ambiguity throws light on the nature of the sacrament. I would like to argue that the sacrament of baptism in its full and proper sense includes both the formal initiation into the Christian faith and the ongoing state of being baptised, of constantly receiving the gift of faith.

I realise of course that in common usage what is signified by the rite is just entry into Christian life. But I would argue that the whole theology of a baptismal 'character' developed precisely to ensure that we do not confine the sacrament of baptism to a single event. It might well have happened that in ordinary usage the term 'sacrament of baptism' retained the dual reference, to event and to state, as happened in the case of the term 'sacrament of matrimony'. The theology of the enduring 'character' of baptism, if it is properly understood, can be seen as a different way of conceptualising the same dual aspect, namely, that the signified reality of baptism is both an event and a state. At the popular level the main stress may have been on the point that the permanent character ensured that the sacrament could not be repeated. But this raises the question *why* the sacrament could not be repeated. And the answer is that it is in some sense an enduring reality. The patristic image of a seal conveys the same insight. Unfortunately, the theology of the character, at least in its popular presentation, has not succeeded very well in making people aware of the ongoing reality of baptism. Perhaps it is inevitable that people took it in a rather legal sense, as some special mark. What was not sufficiently understood was that this 'mark' was in fact the immersion in the life of Christ.

Extended meaning of baptism

It seems to me that at this stage it might still be possible to communicate to people a richer understanding of baptismal character and in this way to take account of the New Testament emphasis on the continuing reality of baptism. However, in order to reach out from the Catholic side towards the Pentecostal position I am proposing an alternative approach. It is not a matter of rejecting the traditional notion of a baptismal character. Rather it is a different way of conceptualising the same basic insight. Apart from its ecumenical value there are good intrinsic reasons for adopting this approach. It offers, I think, a better light on the real meaning of sacramental life in the Church. And it seems to me to be somewhat closer to the biblical conception of baptism.

The suggestion I am making is that we should adopt an extended meaning for the phrase 'sacrament of baptism'. It would then include both the rite of baptism (a single event) and the ongoing reality of continually being immersed by the Spirit in the life of Christ with all its implications. This ongoing reality is precisely what I have identified as the core of 'baptism in the Spirit'. So if we take 'baptism' in the extended sense proposed we can reconcile the key element in Pentecostal spirituality with the New Testament teaching and with the traditional conception of baptism.

Adult experience of faith

The key point in this approach is that the proper meaning of baptism is to be understood only in terms of the kind of conscious adult experience of Christian living which we noted when we examined the New Testament meaning of 'baptism in the Spirit'. This is not an argument against infant baptism. But it is an argument against taking infant baptism as the basic term of reference for understanding what baptism is all about. So I think it would be very misleading to argue that the essential reality symbolised by the rite of baptism cannot be a conscious experience of Christian faith since a baptised infant has no such conscious experience. Rather we should take as the norm the fully conscious experience of faith spoken of in the New Testament; this can then be trimmed down in the case of infants or children to take account of their capacities.

Following out this principle it makes sense to say that the enduring reality of baptism includes an awareness of being enfolded in the love of the Father, a consciousness of surrendering in faith to Christ the Lord, a sense of being guided and prayed in by the Holy Spirit, an experience of belonging to the community of believers and of sharing with them in the mission of Christ, and all the other features of authentic Christian living which we have listed earlier. This continuing reality of sacramental baptism is just the same as 'being baptised in the Spirit' when this is taken in the primary sense we suggested, namely, as an enduring state rather than just as an event.

What then of the baptised adult Christian who has no such Christian experience? I would say that apart from some special situations which we shall note later, such a person has either abandoned Christian faith or has never personally appropriated it. When that person was baptised as an infant he or she was formally taken into the Christian community and given the graces of Christian life in so far as an infant can be given them. But that does not dispense the individual from taking a personal stance in life, from accepting the offered gift of conscious faith. Rejection of Christian faith may be formal and explicit or it may be embodied in the pattern of the person's life without any dramatic act of repudiation. Personal appropriation of the faith may also be a gradual and implicit process; in such a case there may not be a very highly charged awareness of the implications of Christian living; but the adult Christian believer must be a conscious believer in some sense.

Faith and grace in infants

If conscious adult faith is the primary reality symbolised by the rite of baptism can we claim that infant baptism really effects what the rite symbolises? Yes, with some qualifications. The infant is really and formally incorporated into the Christian community, the Body of Christ. This real (ontological) change may be conceptualised in different ways, one of which is the Scholastic conception of sanctifying grace as an 'entitative habitus'. But however we express the reality we must not fall into the trap of concluding that there is no fundamental difference between grace and faith in the infant and in the adult. The total gratuitousness of God's gift is a feature common to grace in adult and infant. But we cannot ignore the obvious differences between infant and adult or assume that such differences are of no real consequence as far as Christian faith is concerned.

Just as theologians now explain the reality of original sin in the infant without positing any personal guilt in the child, so we must explain the reality of grace and faith in the infant without positing any obviously conscious experience of them. The easy, and wrong, way to do so is to define grace and faith as realities independent of consciousness. It is wrong because it leaves the most important aspects of adult Christian faith in the area of accidentals or consequences. The more difficult but more authentic way of approaching the problem is to accept that both 'grace' and 'faith' are not univocal terms but analogous ones. In their full and adequate meaning they refer to the conscious Christian living of the adult. But they also have a genuine meaning as referring to an infant.

Just as the infant is accepted as a true human person even at an age when he or she is unable to perform the kind of acts that distinguish a human from an animal, so too we accept the child as a real Christian (having grace and faith) before he or she can experience this consciously—at least in any obvious way. It is not simply a matter of social status, i.e. that the child is accepted as belonging to the Christian community. There is also a psychological component. The infant is conscious in a human way from the first; the enormous importance of one's very earliest impressions and memories show clearly that there is continuity between the experience of the infant and the adult. We might say that the child is passively human long before he or she becomes actively human. And the same may be said of the experience of grace. The graces that exist in the child are from the first oriented towards full conscious experience; and the development is from the inchoate to the explicit rather than from the unconscious to the conscious. All this is far more easy to accept if we can stop thinking of grace as a 'thing' added to human nature and see it as the context in which human life is actually lived—namely, the context of interpersonal relationships with the Father, with Christ and with the Spirit.

Reconcile with New Testament?

But is it not true that the New Testament does not envisage any instance of a baptised person having to wait some time before experiencing baptism in the Spirit? Are we then contradicting the New Testament? No, it is simply a matter of developing its teaching by taking account of factors which did not apply in the situation envisaged by the New Testament writers. One such factor is infant baptism. It is likely that at least some infants were baptised in New Testament times but the passages we have considered were referring to adults, not infants.

Another factor which does not seem to have been envisaged in these passages is the possibility that somebody baptised as an infant can fail to move decisively into an adult faith; one can drift along for some time accepting Christian doctrine and morals in a rather passive way—and such a person can hardly have the kind of experiences associated with being baptised in the Spirit. The likelihood of this kind of situation arising is greatly increased by a factor we noted in an earlier chapter—a process of distortion which leads many people to have very low expectations[5] about what faith should do for them; these low expectations come from accepting as normal a very watered-down version of Christianity.

There is one other factor which does not seem to have been envisaged by New Testament writers. It is the fact that a living, deeply felt experience of Christian faith may at times be blocked in a particular individual because of some psychological illness, such as depression or excessive anxiety. In such cases the person may not be able to experience the proper effects of Christian faith until an inner healing of the psyche, emotions and memory takes place.

All of these cases, however frequent they may be, can be seen as exceptions to the general principle. This principle is that, fundamentally, sacramental baptism and baptism in the Spirit have the same meaning, namely an enduring state of living Christian faith, a state symbolised and formally initiated by the rite of baptism.

Reversal of the order

The primary relationship between the rite of baptism and the state of being baptised in the Spirit is the relation between a sacramental sign and the reality it signifies. This leaves room for a gap in time between the performance of the rite and the full flowering of the reality signified, as we have just explained. But it also means that there can be a reversal of the normal order. Perhaps the clearest instance of such a reversal is the case of the conversion of Cornelius and his family recounted in chapter ten of the Acts of the Apostles. There the reality signified preceded the sacramental sign. I would assume that something similar (though less dramatic) would take place in the case of most adult converts.

In fact in areas where people are asked to do a catechumenate of a year or two, and are deeply involved in Christian living during that period, one would almost say that the Church has institutionalised a situation where baptism in the Spirit ought to precede the rite of baptism. And rightly, too, for life is larger than logic—and there is need for such a period of growth into the full life of the Christian community.

The notion of baptism of desire was developed by the theologians to explain the real Christian faith and love of such people. But the full implications of it were often overlooked. The theory was used mostly to cover hard cases such as that of catechumens who died before they could be baptised. But I am not sure that religious educators have taken sufficient account of the fact that the ordinary catechumen can be expected to have genuine

Christian faith. On the other hand the Church does accept as real Christians groups who do not practise the rite of baptism; for instance The Society of Friends ('Quakers'). This helps us to avoid an exaggerated realism in understanding the purpose of the rite of baptism. The rite is essentially a public, formal, symbolic act; and the nature of such acts is that they allow for a gap between the rite and what it symbolises and formally initiates. The formal initiation of any human activity may take place before or after its effective, practical beginning. It is not that the formal initiation is just a pretence. It is as real as the other but in a different order of reality.

'Release of the Spirit'?

This way of understanding the relationship between baptism in the Spirit and the rite of baptism enables us to avoid a whole set of difficulties which usually crop up when Catholics try to explain what is involved in baptism in the Spirit. Traditional Catholic teaching has always insisted that the baptised infant has already received grace and the Holy Spirit. How then explain the dramatic breakthrough which plays such a central role for Pentecostalists and 'charismatics'? Catholics cannot accept the classical Pentecostalist interpretation, which contrasts this 'baptism in the Spirit' with 'mere water baptism'. The most common approach is to see the breakthrough as a 'release of the Spirit', who was given long ago in infant baptism but did not have the opportunity to become really effective until now.[6] The word 'release' may also be applied to the gifts or powers of the Spirit, given in baptism but now becoming fully operative.

This word 'release' has certain advantages. Firstly, it establishes a link between the rite of baptism and baptism in the Spirit; and ensures that the rite is not dismissed as unimportant. Secondly, the word fits in well with the emphasis given by all in the Pentecostal tradition to a sudden breakthrough. However, this approach can be criticised on a number of grounds. It seems to operate on a rather crudely realistic conception of the effect of the sacramental rite in an attempt to defend it against the danger of dismissing it as merely symbolic; whereas it is through its formal and symbolic character that the rite has a real effect—

D

as we have tried to show. Furthermore the word 'release' suggests a crudely realistic conception of the presence of the Spirit 'in' the person but somehow unable to operate freely there.[7]

'Emergence'?

Some of the more sophisticated theological explanations of 'baptism in the Spirit' try to avoid the difficulty by saying that what is occurring is a 'breaking forth' or 'emergence' into conscious experience of the Spirit or his gifts; prior to this the Spirit and his gifts would have been present but not consciously experienced.[8]

There is something to be said for this way of speaking but in my opinion it depends on a conception of the human person (or human nature) which is not a very happy one. It is as though the person were thought of as rather like an iceberg, with the small tip above water being the conscious part and the large part below the water-line being the unconscious part. After infant baptism the Holy Spirit, and/or the gifts and powers of the Spirit, can be considered as present in the non-conscious part. 'Baptism in the Spirit' will then be interpreted as the emergence or breakthrough of the Spirit or his gifts and powers from the unconscious to the conscious sector of the person.

Though superficially attractive, this model of the human person and of the presence of the Spirit seems to me to be quite inadequate. It is far too simple to divide the person into conscious and non-conscious sectors. As I suggested in a previous chapter[9] there are several different levels of conscious and pre-conscious life in the human person, e.g. the level of biological-chemical reactions, the level of psycho-motor reflexes, the level of spontaneous consciousness and the level of deliberate consciousness. It does not make much sense to think of the Spirit, or of his gifts or graces, being somehow present for years in one of the 'lower' levels and then breaking through to the conscious levels. So we must assume that what is in question is some kind of ontological substratum of the person which can be the abode of the Spirit and his gifts, powers and graces. Frankly, I don't know what that would mean; I cannot accept that kind of model of human nature. For one thing it seems to imply that what is 'really real' in the person lies in a region that is quite beyond the reach of consciousness. Whereas I think that the real core of the human person lies at the point where the conscious ego is linked to those creative depths in us which are only partly under our conscious control—but are by no means an inert substratum. In the next chapter I shall explore this point more fully.

In the understanding of human consciousness which I accept there is no room for the idea that the Holy Spirit or his gifts are hidden in some secret region of the soul and can later emerge into consciousness. We should not then imagine the emergence of the Spirit from an unconscious metaphysical substratum in us. Rather we can think of baptism in the Spirit in terms of newly-established links between deliberate faith and our spontaneous feelings, desires, attitudes and hopes. This results in great peace and freedom, a sense of integration, and a spontaneous desire to pray and to correspond with the guidance of the Spirit.

Gelpi and Laurentin

At this point it may be helpful to refer to the views of two theologians whose conception of baptism in the Spirit is in broad agreement with the one I have outlined. The first of these is the well-known French author René Laurentin who has written an important study entitled *Catholic Pentecostalism*.[10] In the course of it he has a helpful section on baptism in the Spirit.

Laurentin's approach is very refreshing. He reacts against any attempt to equate the formulas of the Bible with those of later sacramental theology.[11] And he maintains that it would be wrong to strive for a total harmonisation of different theological traditions.[12] He does not object to the use of the term 'baptism in the Spirit'. To the objection that it is confusing and ambiguous, he replies that greater ambiguities are already present in our sacramental theology.[13] The term is useful because it brings us back to the realities of Christian experience and the pastoral need for those who were baptised in infancy 'to come into genuine contact with God by awakening faith and love in their hearts.'[14]

Laurentin maintains that the experience of baptism in the

Spirit 'does indeed have a place in the most classical type of Catholic theology . . . and no little light is shed on the experience by such a theology.'[15] He approaches the task in two stages. Firstly, he rejects the kind of theology of baptism which takes infant baptism as the norm and consequently stresses the 'ontology of the objective grace of baptism' while paying no attention to the experience of the recipient.[16] Secondly, he proposes a theory based on the ancient distinction between (1) the *sacramentum,* i.e. the external rite or sacramental sign, (2) the *res et sacramentum,* i.e. the effect which is also a sign, and (3) the *res,* i.e. the ultimate effect or reality.[17] Laurentin insists that the *res* or ultimate effect and reality of baptism is something existential. (This means it is not just something in the ontological order beyond consciousness.) So he concludes that baptism in the Spirit is the *res* or ultimate effect and reality aimed at in the sacrament of baptism. Laurentin's conclusion is in very close agreement with the view I have proposed. It would have been very interesting to see it developed in more detail, particularly in regard to the place of the *res et sacramentum* (the effect which is also a sign). But unfortunately he merely remarks that this latter is incorporation into the Church, the Body of Christ. He does not attempt to explain what baptismal grace means in an infant.

Another writer whose approach is rather close to the one I have outlined is Donald L. Gelpi. Writing in 1971 he defended the conception of 'Spirit-baptism' while insisting that it is not a sacrament. For him it meant the prayer of the group over the person and also the response of God to that prayer, 'particularly in its experienced consequences'.[18] A few years later he added: 'Spirit-baptism is a life-time process. It cannot be equated with any single graced experience . . .'[19] Although seeing it as a process, he thinks that every Christian is called, as Christ was, to 'a moment of decisive "charismatic" breakthrough'.[20] This 'moment' may be reached gradually or suddenly. It changes a person's life, bringing intensification and personalisation of baptismal faith.

Gelpi's position harmonises well with that which I have outlined. His emphasis in his later book on baptism in the Spirit as a process is especially welcome. But I think one has to go a step further and see the process as itself an entry into a state; otherwise there are difficulties about explaining the relationship between sacramental baptism and baptism in the Spirit.

Alternative approaches

Important studies of baptism in the Spirit have been made by two outstanding theologians—Simon Tugwell and Francis A. Sullivan. Neither of them are happy with the use of the term. The fact that their conclusion on this point differs from mine can be explained in the light of the more extended meaning I have given to this term and to the understanding of sacramental baptism. We do not disagree to any significant extent in our understanding of the event of baptism in the Spirit as a religious experience. Nor do we disagree in our understanding of the teaching of the New Testament.

It seems that the basic objection of Tugwell to the use of the term baptism in the Spirit is that it would suggest a once-for-all happening; whereas Tugwell insists that 'there is a diversity of experiences of the Spirit'.[21] He maintains that Pentecostalism 'has so over-objectified one particular kind of experience of the Spirit, that it has almost no account to give of others'.[22] This is perhaps something of an exaggeration, but it does point to a major weakness in the Pentecostalist and 'charismatic' spirituality. The remedy proposed by Tugwell is to abandon the term 'baptism in the Spirit', to recognise a variety of different kinds of experiences of the Spirit, and to borrow other terms (e.g. the 'manifestation of baptism') to designate the decisive 'emergence into consciousness' of the gifts of the Spirit. I have proposed a different solution to the same problem: that we recognise that baptism in the Spirit is primarily a state rather than a single event.

The approach of Sullivan is an interesting one. His objection to the use of the term 'baptism in the Spirit' can be summarised in two points. Firstly, we must say on scriptural grounds that every baptised Christian has been baptised in the Spirit; but, secondly, people in the Pentecostal tradition use the term in such a way as to imply that most Christians have not been baptised in the Spirit.[23] Sullivan's way out of the difficulty is to give a more neutral name to the religious event usually called 'baptism in the Spirit'. At first he simply calls it 'the pentecostal experience'. He then goes on to interpret this as a new kind of presence of the Spirit and a new relationship to the Spirit. As a technical term to describe what is involved he proposes a word from St Thomas Aquinas, *innovatio*, to which the English equivalent would be 'a new outpouring of the Holy Spirit' for the person's 'renewal in the Spirit'.[24] The most distinctive point in Sullivan's approach is that he understands this new coming or outpouring to be a charismatic gift independent of the sacraments: '. . . a Catholic need not try to interpret the pentecostal experience merely in relation to Baptism and Confirmation, as an "actuation", "release", "manifestation" or "reviviscence" of gifts already received in those sacraments'.[25]

This approach of Sullivan is very helpful in many respects. He succeeds in taking account of the basic Pentecostal insight—namely, the importance of a conscious immersion in the life of Christ. At the same time he avoids the difficulties experienced by most Catholic writers in linking this with the sacrament of baptism. This he achieves by cutting the link with baptism. However, this has the effect of reducing what Sullivan calls 'the pentecostal experience' to the status of an optional extra. It becomes a second blessing which a Christian *may* receive, but not, apparently, a gift that every normal adult Christian must have. That conclusion is quite correct if what is in question is a sudden and dramatic experience of breakthrough. But if what is in question is the ongoing state of being consciously immersed in the life and love of God, then it cannot be considered an optional extra for the Christian. For, as I have tried to show, the New Testament considers this to be the norm for the Christian, and this is what is symbolised and formally initiated in the rite of baptism. So I prefer to retain a link with the rite of baptism[26] and to retain the term 'baptism in the Spirit', provided these are rightly understood.

Comparison

We have considered four different ways of approaching this whole question. Firstly, there is the strict Pentecostalist view which contrasts 'mere water baptism' with 'baptism in the Spirit', and which sees the latter as a second blessing, given subsequent to evangelical conversion which is seen as the beginning of real Christian life. This view proves indefensible on scriptural grounds.

Secondly, there is Sullivan's view which does not accept the term 'baptism in the Spirit' but accepts what generally goes under that term and gives it another name—a new outpouring of the Spirit for renewal; this it explains as a charismatic gift given to some Christians but having no special link with the sacrament of baptism. This approach seems to minimise the importance for every Christian of coming, either suddenly or gradually, to experience the effects associated with being baptised in the Spirit.

Thirdly, there is the approach which thinks in terms of a 'release of the Spirit' or of an 'emergence into conscious experience' of his gifts already received in baptism but hitherto dormant in some deep level of the soul. This approach seems to imply a conception of the human person which is not very convincing.

Finally, there is the approach which I have suggested in this chapter and which I now very briefly summarise. It involves seeing a fundamental unity in the sacrament of baptism. Within this unity one discerns the sign aspect and the signified aspect. The sign aspect is the rite of baptism, reinforced and kept alive by such things as the renewal of baptismal promises or the use of holy water. The signified reality is itself two-fold—the entry into the life of Christ and the ongoing immersion in it. The rite is the formal sacramental expression of this two-fold reality; and to be baptised is to be baptised in the Spirit. But it is only when a person has a conscious experience of being immersed in the love of God that the full signified reality of baptism is present. When that is present one can say the person is in the state called baptism in the Spirit.

This latter approach seems to me to have certain advantages over the other approaches:

—It offers a deeper and broader interpretation of the experience generally known as 'baptism in the Spirit', situating it within a context in which one can say that the same effects can occur through a gradual process.

—It relates baptism in the Spirit more successfully to the rite of baptism.

—It is based on a model of human nature and human consciousness which is more credible.

—It is more faithful to the data of the New Testament which must of course remain the standard by which the validity of any particular approach is to be judged.

However, this approach calls for two adjustments to our thinking, two extensions of the meaning of words or phrases which are at present unduly limited in their common usage. Firstly, it requires that we understand baptism in the Spirit as primarily a state rather than a single dramatic event. Secondly, it requires that we understand the sacrament of baptism as an enduring reality, in the sense that the reality signified is the state of living in Christ as well as entry into that state. In each case I have tried to present cogent reasons for this extension of meaning; and I have suggested that the extended meaning is already implicit in present usage. If these reasons are accepted and if the meanings are extended in the way suggested, then we have found a way to rescue the term 'baptism in the Spirit' from unacceptable Pentecostalist implications. This could be a helpful contribution to the ongoing ecumenical convergence of the Catholic, Protestant and Pentecostal spiritualities.

PART FOUR

LETTING GO

7. LETTING GO TO GOD

People giving testimony about their experience of being baptised in the Spirit very frequently emphasise the point that for them it involved total surrender to God. This is how one well-known Catholic Scripture scholar describes it:

> . . . though *I* may have had the Holy Spirit, *he* was far from having *me*. The crazy 'baptism of the Holy Spirit' of which the charismatics spoke . . . might be just the thing I needed—and feared—the most: the gift of *being given* to the Lord in a new way, a way in which I would let *him* take over the controls.[1]

A Presbyterian author maintains that the human contribution required by God is 'a kind of *letting go*' which he explains as follows:

> . . . combined with openness, eagerness, and the like, there is surrender of all that one is and has to the movement of God's Spirit . . . it is the offering of self as a total sacrifice. This includes more than the dedication of one's conscious existence through an act of will; it also refers to the large, even hidden, area of one's unconscious life.[2]

Kinds of letting go

The phrase 'letting go' seems to me to indicate the fundamental attitude or disposition needed in order that a person enter into or live fully in the state of being baptised in the Spirit as described in chapter 2 above. It is necessary, however, to distinguish between various kinds of letting go. For convenience I shall speak of four distinct situations;[3] but it must be noted

that the boundaries between these different categories are by no
means rigid, so there may be a good deal of overlapping.

The most obvious kind of self-surrender takes place in the
conversion of an overt sinner. Here the letting go involves
repentance which means a rejection of sin and a seeking of God's
forgiveness. There is a conversion in the full scriptural sense, a
metanoia which should normally permeate every sector of the
convert's life and consciousness.

A somewhat different kind of letting go is called for in the case
of many people who have long ago turned from a life of sin.
They may become aware that they have been holding back on
God, refusing something he is asking of them. It is not a question
of some big sin but of some item that might have seemed quite
trivial. It has become important as a test-case or symbol of
willingness to submit fully to God. In this situation the person
becomes vividly aware of the truth of St John of the Cross's
image: it does not require a heavy rope to prevent a bird from
flying freely; even a silk thread, so long as it remains unbroken,
will hold him back.

The third situation in which a letting go is called for involves
a rather different type of moral crisis. It is the situation of a
person who has not until now taken any very clear stance in life.
This is a crisis of growth. It should be the culmination of what
might be called a time of moral adolescence—which might come
years after the person had legally come of age. The classical
studies on the psychology of conversion made by William James[4]
seem to me to have taken their data very much from conversions
of this kind. In fact the pattern is quite similar to that of the
conversion of an overt sinner. The person feels overwhelmed by
sin and feels the need to be rescued. An observer may think that
the convert's talk about sin is an exaggeration. But I think this
sense of sin has an objective basis: a certain moral selfishness is
more or less inevitable in the person who has not yet dedicated
himself or herself to somebody or something outside themselves.
The convert feels called to make a definite break with a self-
centred past. It means abandoning the self that he or she had
been up to now. The most difficult part is the letting go of what-
ever securities had been built up, and venturing forward into
unknown territory. The decisive step is taken through an act of

attitude of self-surrender which allows God to take over the central role in one's life.

A moral crisis is a feature common to all three of the kinds of letting go described above. But I want now to examine in some detail a fourth kind of self-surrender, one where the focal point does not seem to be moral in the usual sense. It is not strictly a matter of making some basic option. Nor is it a question of doing or avoiding some particular kind of action. The situation I have in mind here is that of the person whom I called earlier 'the dutiful Christian'.[5] This is an earnest and virtuous believer, not merely orthodox in belief but really good in behaviour, one who is determined to discover and follow the will of God. I am not thinking here of people who are guilty of a smug pharisee-like assurance of their own virtue; but of Christians who are well aware of their weakness and rely on God to the best of their ability.

Having lived for years with a duty-full experience of the faith, such a Christian may gradually or more suddenly become aware of an important dimension which seems to be missing from that faith. The missing dimension involves a deeper kind of self-surrender to God. The person begins to suspect that only out of such a complete handing over to God can come deep peace and joy, unselfish service of others and real Christian freedom of spirit. So the person really *wants* to let go to all this.

Religious rather than moral

But how is one to go about it? There is no specific moral issue on which one experiences a holding back; it is something far more vague and general. In this sense the problem is not experienced as a moral one—though it certainly has moral implications since a breakthrough would in fact transform one's moral life. But the central focus is religious rather than moral, in so far as it has to do with a general attitude to life and particularly to God.

It is exceptionally difficult in this situation to pin down some act or line of action which would constitute one's letting go to God. To say that what is required is an act of will is to miss the point. It is quite true that if I really will to give myself to God then

I have in a certain sense already surrendered myself to him. But the 'earnest Christian' has been doing just that for years! And now it seems that something more is required. Perhaps the difficulty can be expressed by saying that the 'I' that offers myself is not a totally integrated and timeless self—and so neither is the 'I' that I offer. How then am I to gather myself together as both giver and gift?

People who find the answer to this question say that their letting go involved an abandonment of the 'persona' they had built up over the years. In many respects this is similar to the letting go I last referred to—the crisis of growth which brings moral adolescence to an end. But in that case the personality is still pliable; there is question of taking a deeply personal option for the first time. In the situation considered here, the step is more difficult because one is asked to let go of a fully-formed personality. This personality incorporates all one's beliefs, attitudes and commitments. It is one's public and private self-image. It is the product of a life-time—the past carried into the present. To let it go is a kind of suicide, a step over the cliff into unreality. Such a step is unthinkable and unimaginable until it is actually done. In so far as it is something actually done, it is a leap of total, abandoning trust. But in fact it is experienced less as something one *does* than as a *gift*, something done by God for and in the person.

This account goes a long way towards explaining how beginning to speak in tongues can for many people be an effective focus and a powerful symbol of letting go. It is a deliberate step out of the ordered, rational world structured by one's own language, a step into apparent unintelligibility.[6] Yet the step once taken is experienced as bringing one not into total chaos but into a world which does have meaning: for the strange sounds are experienced as language in some sense. But the language and the order are not of one's own making; this is a world where one is no longer the master. The person has let go and been carried into a new world which is experienced as pure gift.

The description just given may seem to refer to a sudden and dramatic breakthrough. But that is only one of the ways in which the letting go can occur. The self-surrender may also be gradual and cumulative.[7] It is no less effective if it occurs like this—indicating that what is in question is not some passing emotional experience but a significant transformation of personality.

Saved by faith

The classic religious description of the act of letting go to God is 'salvation by faith'. Its first moment is the recognition of helplessness, of inability to save oneself. Then comes a second moment which is a cry for rescue. The third moment is an act of total trust, an acceptance that one is loved, accepted, saved, quite unconditionally and without reference to one's merits. In fact it is precisely the abandonment of all pretensions of merit that opens the person up to receive the gift: '. . . for by grace you have been saved through faith; and this is not your own doing, it is the gift of God—not because of works, lest any man should boast' (*Eph.* 2 : 8-9). 'Therefore, since we are justified by faith, we have peace with God through our Lord Jesus Christ. Through him we have access to this grace in which we stand . . .' (*Rom.* 5 : 1-2).

The dutiful Christian is somebody in whom this process of salvation by faith has already taken place in some degree; but a significant part of the process remains to be achieved. I think it is inaccurate to say that the new kind of letting go merely adds something accidental to the person's faith and salvation. But it is equally inaccurate to maintain that it is essential in the sense that until it occurs the person has no real saving faith. Life is larger than logic. Not every Christian is a fully integrated and unified personality. So there can be a self-surrender to God at one level which leaves room for a different, more existential, kind of letting go—and this is what we are discussing.

Psychological explanation?

I think it is important to try to locate more precisely what is involved in the letting go that turns a dutiful Christian into somebody who has entered the state of being baptised in the Spirit. For if we can pin-point it then we have a better chance of achieving it—or rather of disposing ourselves to receive it as a gift.

'Dutiful Christians' are people who have done their best to turn to God. But they find that the joy, peace and freedom that should characterise the Christian life is largely absent from their lives. When such people let go to God it seems to put them in touch with a deep source of life, hope and joy; it gives them a new integration of character which is a source of peace and quiet strength. We say, quite rightly, that all this is the gift of God. But it seems to me that if God is really transcendent we should expect that he would operate through some secondary causality.[8] In that case it should be possible to give a psychological explanation of the process.

This does not mean that we are trying to explain away God's gift, his intervention in our lives. Quite the contrary. It means that we hold for a constant and intimate involvement of God rather than an episodic intervention from outside. We experience God acting within us through his providential ordering of the events and processes that take place around and within us. And it is the gift of faith that enables us to recognise that providence and put our trust in it.

A hymn that is popular with people in the Charismatic Renewal speaks of peace and hope 'flowing like a river, flowing out of you and me, flowing out into the desert, setting all the captives free'. There is an echo here of many scriptural texts, but especially two from St John's gospel: 'The water I shall give will be an inner spring always welling up for eternal life' (*John* 4:14); and 'From within him shall flow rivers of living water' (*John* 7:37).[9] This imagery is particularly apt for conveying the experience of those who have let go in the sense we are speaking of. They feel within them a new source of life and hope and strength. Is it possible to give a psychological explanation of the discovery of a 'fountain of life' within them? I think it is, with the help of the writings of the noted psychologist Ira Progoff.

Progoff's psychology

With a background in the psychology of Jung, Progoff has developed the theory and practice of psychotherapy to a point where his primary concern is not the healing of mental illness but the growth of normal people. So he is dissatisfied with the terms 'psycho-analysis' and 'psycho-therapy' and prefers to speak of 'psyche-evoking'—that is, the use of techniques which can put people in touch with 'the deep psychic fount of creativity within man'.[10] He believes that in Western society we have concentrated so much on intellectual development that we have to a great extent lost touch with the deeper, more intuitional dimension of the human spirit. He says:

> There are levels of reality within us that are much greater than our analytical minds can know. Nonetheless, we can make them accessible to our awareness so that they become channels by which we reconnect ourselves to the great sources of life. Evoking the depths of ourselves is a way to the renewal of our humanity.[11]

We are not concerned here with the techniques used by Progoff but with the results of a successful use of them. The person is enabled to make 'contact . . . with the underlying principle of the psyche'.[12] The effect is a transformation of the atmosphere in which life is lived, a new quality of existence.[13] This gives the person 'a sense of meaning and connection' in life; it gives 'an inner perspective', 'special knowledge and support' and the strength to endure frustrations.[14] The sense of connectedness to life goes a long way towards eliminating anxieties; it can neutralise feelings of competitiveness and fears of failure.[15] Deep sources of creativity in the personality are opened up and new inspirations and insights are admitted.[16] There is also the ability to sense the direction in which the person is developing; and this gives a sense of inner guidance which is enormously important in human survival and growth.[17]

The social effects of this new contact with the depths of the psyche are just as remarkable as the purely personal ones. There is a new openness to others because one has entered into 'the dimension of life on which people are joined together rather than separated'.[18] Progoff says:

> Love depends upon the capacity to reach beneath the surface of persons, to feel and touch the seed of life that is hidden

there. . . . Creative love becomes psychologically possible
when the work of sensitising the depths of personality has been
carried through.[19]

This kind of love establishes a deep bond of sympathy which
enables one to sense what the other person wants or needs and
to respond almost intuitively. If one is working with a group one
has the power to sense its moods and unexpressed desires.

In addition to the personal and social effects there can also be
a certain cosmic effect. One attains a sense of connectedness even
with the non-human world, an experience of being in tune with
its rhythm. This can give one a certain intuitive accuracy even
in the operation of machinery.[20]

'Psychic conversion'

Progoff's work helps us to understand why people who try to
live on the basis of a purely intellectual approach to life run into
so many psychological difficulties. They do not have free access
to the deep sources of vitality and energy within them. They
may have a theory about the meaning of life but they lack a vivid
experience of meaning and purpose.[21] This gives rise to insecurity and anxiety.[22] They are also deficient in basic sympathy
with other people and the whole environment. The result is a
sense of isolation, which may find expression in aggression. If
the aggression is repressed by a deliberate moral effort its
destructive potential may be turned inward to damage the personality in a variety of ways.

People in this situation are in need of a major psychological
re-orientation, what some recent theorists would call a 'psychic
conversion'. It is a breakthrough to a deeper level of the self
than the rational-discursive ego. At this deeper level one can tap
the springs of life, hope, strength and meaning, and discover a
source of harmony with and in life.

What is the relationship between this psychic conversion and
the transformation that takes place when a dutiful Christian
begins to live in the state of being baptised in the Spirit? Let us
consider a variety of different answers one could give to this
vital question:

—One could say that the similarities are merely coincidental, that there are two quite different realities, one taking place in the Christian supernatural order, the other in the merely natural order. Modern theology has shown the weakness of such a position, as I pointed out briefly in chapter 2 above.[23]

—One could again insist that the similarities are not significant, since there is question of two different levels of reality, one being religious or spiritual, the other being merely at the level of psychology. This approach is quite unsatisfactory: it creates or presupposes a barrier between the spiritual order and everyday secular life; and the resultant dichotomy can hardly be overcome.

—One could, on the other hand, identify the two processes entirely, saying that in one case the breakthrough is described in Christian language while in the other case the same process is described in terms borrowed from Jungian psychology. I believe that this oversimplifies the case, but it is much closer to the truth than the previous two answers.

—One can try to show that the psychological breakthrough is a part or aspect of what occurs when the 'dutiful' Christian succeeds in letting go to God. This is the view I would like to defend. But it leaves me with the difficult task of explaining what the latter adds to the former.

Faith interpretation

Where the psychological breakthrough occurs in the kind of context provided by the Charismatic Renewal, I believe it will normally constitute entry into the experience of being baptised in the Spirit. No additional content is required, for in this case the psychological process is at the same time the religious process. What the Christian faith adds is not some further content but a context and interpretation of the process. Invoking the distinction, introduced in chapter 3, between intrinsic and imposed meaning, I would say that the faith enables one to give a specifically Christian imposed meaning to the psychological process. Faith enables one to see the whole process as a special gift of God. It gives one the ability to interpret the new contact with the depths of the self as a new and deeper encounter with God.

And in faith one experiences the act of self-surrender to the deeper self as a real letting go to God. In saying all this I am simply applying the conception of faith as interpretation which I proposed in chapter 1.[24]

It may be argued against this approach that the Progoff-type of psychological breakthrough can take place in people who see no Christian meaning in it, and even in people who have no religious faith at all. This objection can be answered by considering the nuances of the relationship between intrinsic and imposed meanings, as outlined earlier.[25] Let us consider three different cases:

—The first case is where the psychological breakthrough is Christian in everything but name. It opens up the person to the Transcendent in submission and trust, even though the appropriate Christian words are lacking. The absence of an appropriate language is serious, but not so serious as to prevent the emergence of an implicit or lived faith.

—The second case is where the psychological breakthrough occurs in a context which gives it a quite misleading imposed meaning. For instance, the Christian interpretation may be replaced by a pantheistic or monistic theory or some kind of naturalistic mysticism. Such a faulty interpretation can have a feed-back effect on the process itself. For instance it could lead the person to filter out certain elements which a Christian interpretation would encourage—e.g. a deeply felt instinct to use prayer of petition.

—A third case is where the psychological breakthrough takes place in somebody who is not morally converted. In such a situation the experience is liable to have a character or tone that is more aesthetic than religious—since aesthetic openness co-exists somewhat more easily with lack of moral conversion than does religious openness. This may well be the situation of certain poets and artists who combine moral selfishness with an aesthetic sensitivity which borders on the religious. But it can even happen that a morally unconverted person is deeply religious; it's untidy, illogical—but it happens! There is a fascinating ambiguity in Patrick Kavanagh's little poem:

I who have not sown
I too
By God's grace may come to harvest . . .[26]

It could be used by the best of Christians; but it could also be the heart-cry of a religious sinner.

In any case, none of the instances just considered provides a convincing argument against the view I have proposed, namely, that in the proper Christian context, the psychological process of letting go to one's deepest self can be precisely the way one lets go to God.

Meeting God in the depths

Another remarkable poem by Kavanagh includes the following lines:

Lie at the heart of the emotion, time
Has its own work to do. We must not anticipate
Or awaken for a moment. God cannot catch us
Unless we stay in the unconscious room
Of our hearts. We must be nothing,
Nothing that God may make us something,
We must not touch the immortal material
We must not day-dream tomorrow's judgement—
God must be allowed to surprise us.[27]

I would like to reflect on why it is that 'God cannot catch us unless we stay in the unconscious room'. Eric Voegelin gives a very helpful account of the relationship between the conscious ego and 'the depth'. We must, he says, recognise that

the conscious subject occupies only a small area in the soul. Beyond this area extends the reality of the soul, vast and darkening in depth, whose movements reach into the small area that is organised as the conscious subject. The movements of the depth reverberate in the conscious subject without becoming objects for it.[28]

It is in 'the depth' that one experiences the primordial openness towards what is transcendent: the 'more-than-human dimension' of the soul comes from the terror and the assurance inspired by a 'beyond' which is experienced as at once 'infinitely overpowering' and 'infinitely embracing'.[29] What Voegelin and Kavanagh are speaking of is, I believe, basically that same dimension of depth as Progoff has in mind. And they are saying that in so far as we can speak of meeting God, it is precisely in that depth of us that it occurs. To this I would add that from this centre it can spread out so that the Christian whose faith is fully activated can then see or meet God in every event of life—as I suggested in chapter 1.[30]

But why should 'the depth' be the primordial place for meeting God? The reason is that God is not an object for us, an object to be grasped and evaluated in a purely rational way.[31] He remains beyond, the ineffable. So our response to God has to take place primarily at a deeper level in us than the sphere of ordinary knowledge of objects.

Faith

To respond positively to God at this fundamental level of our being is what is meant by 'faith' in its most elementary sense.[32] This response is experienced by the believer as both gift and free choice. But it is not the kind of choice one makes between two clearly defined objects, for at this level there are no distinct objects. In fact down in those depths there is room for only one basic choice—the choice of how we relate to life. Consequently, in this core of us our basic attitude to life (including other people, the world and ourselves) is not separable from our attitude to God. It is through our basic stance in relation to life, to all that is given to us, that our attitude to God is taken up.

In this basic stance in relation to life there is no room for neutrality. There is room, however, for a wide variety of positive or negative attitudes, e.g. hostility, cynicism, opportunism, curious experimentation, wonder, terror, anxious uncertainty, grateful acceptance, desire to dominate, respect, determination to understand and co-operate. The fundamental religious option of a particular individual is his or her selection and 'mix' out of these and similar possible approaches.

It is not a purely arbitrary matter what choice of stance we adopt. There is within the human person a seed or instinct of faith which inclines each of us to make the positive choices.[33] It is true that the forces of evil also impinge on us at this deep level. But however much we discover evil as part of us, the believer judges it to be an intrusion or distortion; the one who follows the instinct of faith is affirming that evil is not part of our deepest God-given self. That deepest self is an openness to life, which branches out into an openness to others, to the world —and to God as their transcendent source. To respond in faith is to be true to the instinct of faith which is the most authentic core of each of us. To have faith in this basic sense is to have adopted one of a range of options which are all positive in relation to life. There is room for variety within this faith; for instance, the faith of one person may be rather action-oriented while that of somebody else may be more receptive and contemplative. But if hostility, sheer terror, or cynicism are the dominant features of our attitude to life, then we cannot be said to have faith.

From anxiety to trust

Having faith is not a matter of all or nothing. In chapter 1 we noted the possibility of variations in comprehensiveness, in explicitness, in intensity and in mood. And I added that there is the possibility of misdirected growth of faith.[34] I wish now to develop this latter point a little. Probably the most common source of distortion in faith—at least in our times and culture— is anxiety. It attacks faith in its deepest core; and it severely limits the extent to which faith radiates outward to permeate the personality. In some people, anxiety is so dominant that it makes faith quite impossible. More commonly it weakens faith and deprives it of some of its more important effects. It causes an imbalance because it interferes far more with the spontaneous aspects of us than with the aspects of personality associated with duty.

The 'dutiful Christian' is somebody whose faith has been stunted in this way. For such a person, to let go to God involves being set free of primordial anxiety. It comes about in the healing experience of being loved unconditionally—an experience of love which evokes an unconditional trust in response. What occurs is so simple and so profound that it is best expressed in the words of a child: 'I ain't frightened', says Anna—and therefore, says her friend, she is able to move out of the centre and let God take over.[35]

Relationship with explicit faith

But how does this experience of faith relate to the explicit, verbalised faith of our creeds, our preaching and our teaching? Certainly it is not a replacement for such explicit faith. The meeting with God in the depths is not a substitute for rational-discursive knowledge about God. Either on its own is inadequate. If we undervalue objectivised discourse about God we tend to get bogged down in subjectivity and vagueness; and the teaching of religion becomes almost impossible. On the other hand, if we confine ourselves to 'objective' discourse, our understanding of God will find no deep roots in experience; and by treating God as an object we shall have missed his reality.

We have been concentrating attention on the deep roots of faith rather than its verbal expression, because in the case of the dutiful Christian the weakness is in the former rather than the latter. To be more precise, we should perhaps say that the weakness is not only in the primordial openness to God in the depths but also in the *links* between the depths of the person and the conscious ego. The person is not deeply in tune with creative sources of life and openness within. The process we have called letting go creates such attunement and allows healing currents of love and trust to flow freely between the conscious ego and the depths. That is why we could say in chapter 3 that when one enters the state of being baptised in the Spirit, one's 'deliberate' faith finds deep echoes and an extraordinary reson-ance at the level of spontaneous consciousness.[36] The new internal lines of communication result in an integration of the personality. And this unified person is governed at every level by faith. The primordial experiences of love and trust find worthy expression in the words of Christian prayer; and the deep meaning of the person's stance in life is articulated in Christian doctrines and moral values. And conversely the whole doctrinal, moral, liturgical and institutional systems of Christianity are experienced as deeply meaningful because they are now plugged in to that person's primordial religious stance.

Techniques

If letting go is ultimately a gift of God, then we must accept that no human techniques can bring it about. However, there are certain ways in which one can become more disposed to want the gift and to receive it. I shall conclude this chapter by considering some of them.

One of the biggest obstacles to our letting go is the tendency to live almost all of the time at a superficial level, occupied and preoccupied by many things. We must take to heart the Lord's words to Martha and give time to 'the one thing that is necessary' (*Luke* 10:42). But when we turn seriously to personal prayer we may find that even there we are 'busy about many things'. It can be very difficult to switch off our racing thoughts and images. In this situation many people are helped by using the technique of rhythmic or repetitive prayer; they repeat the Jesus prayer over and over, or they make use of some other mantra.[37] This can bring about the *bodily* relaxation that is required for contemplative prayer. It has the *psychological* effect of opening up the depths in us while the imagination and mind are tied up with the mantra. And, perhaps most important of all, at the *spiritual* level the adoption of this kind of prayer can represent the self-emptying of the conscious ego. So this kind of prayer can dispose a person to let go to God.

Praying in tongues can have a rather similar effect. Once again here is a way to escape from the tyranny of thought and imagery. This kind of prayer is generally very affective. It can be used to express some deeply-felt religious sentiment. And frequently it not merely expresses deep religious feelings but also evokes them. It can be particularly helpful where a person wishes to make an ardent prayer of praise or petition, but does not want to be distracted from God by focusing attention on any particular 'object' of prayer. When a whole group prays and sings together in tongues the religious atmosphere that is generated can be very powerful indeed. In the past, 'tongues' tended to be seen as the mark that one had been baptised in the Spirit. But I have the impression that more recently it is becoming somewhat more widely accepted as a normal way of praying—which of course it is. It should not be confined to those who have already undergone some dramatic experience of letting go to God; for it can also dispose one to such a self-surrender—or to a more gradual and cumulative type of letting go. The prayer that wells up from the depths of the psyche helps to strengthen the lines of communication between the surface and the depths; and it expresses the submission of the total personality to God.

Another way to dispose oneself to let go to God is to set about listening for the voice of the Spirit. To listen in this way is to surrender oneself as Jesus did: '. . . not my will but thine be done' (*Luke* 22:42). In recent years there has been increased emphasis in the Church on the personal search of the Christian to discover the will of God. Many people are coming to realise for the first time that general laws and directives of authority are not enough; there is need too for specific guidance from the Spirit—and this is given to those believers who really look for it.

Some people in the Charismatic Renewal uncritically borrow from the Pentecostalists ways of trying to *force* the Spirit to answer their questions. For instance they may open the Bible at random to find a reply to the problem they have posed. But the dominant attitude in the Renewal is far more mature and respectful. And one of the most significant developments in the past few years has been the convergence of two spiritualities—the Charismatic and the Ignatian.[38] The latter adds a dimension of depth and rich spiritual subtlety to the Charismatic approach to 'the discernment of spirits'. The Ignatian spirituality lays great stress on being in touch with our own spiritual feelings. The interpretation of these feelings is the basis for discerning our conformity with God. So we are brought back again to the close relationship between being in tune with God and being in tune with one's deepest self.

To help people get in touch with 'the depths', Progoff suggests a technique in which images are encouraged to surface freely into consciousness.[39] This fosters an attitude of psychic openness in the person. That same attitude is to be found in people of the Charismatic Renewal who 'open' themselves for 'prophecy' or 'discernment';[40] though there the context is more explicitly religious. This indicates that to listen for the voice of the Spirit we need to listen to the movements in the depths of our own spirit. What emerges is 'the Spirit himself bearing witness *with* our spirit . . .' (*Rom.* 8 : 16)—a joint message in which it is hard to say what our mediation adds to, or subtracts from, the word of God.

Lest it be thought that this approach is one that explains away the voice of God, I shall quote two passages from Agnes Sanford, who must surely be above suspicion in this regard:

> I have spoken of the voice of the Lord . . . and I have spoken of the subconscious mind giving me the message. Both are true. . . . The actual words may not have been His. But the comprehension of the nature of my trouble was brought up by Him out of the unconscious and was clothed in those words.[41]

Later on, she speaks of listening in private prayer for a message from God: 'This is not the actual voice of God speaking to us in English . . . It is the unconscious mind trying to get across to us some little bit out of the great mysteries that we have briefly touched in spirit.'[42]

In Paul's letter to the Romans it is particularly significant that he makes a causal link between surrendering totally to God and being able to discern his will: 'Offer yourselves as a living sacrifice to God, dedicated to his service and pleasing to him . . . let God transform you inwardly by a complete change of your mind. Then you will be able to know the will of God—what is good, and is pleasing to him and is perfect.' (*Rom.* 12 : 1-2). It is clear then that the more we can let go to our deepest self the more we can discern the voice of the Spirit; and the more we seek his voice, the more we dispose ourselves to receive the gift of surrendering ourselves to God.

One of the most important ways of reaching into 'the depths is by the use of religious symbols. Progoff has published three booklets of 'process meditations' which are built around key images such as water, a well, trees, a cross and a star.[43] They can be used by people of different religions and even by those who profess no religious belief. But these symbolic images are borrowed mostly from the Judaeo-Christian tradition. It is significant that the central images used by Progoff are also prominent in the favourite Scripture texts and hymns of the Charismatic Renewal—and in the 'prophecies' and spontaneous prayers heard in prayer-meetings. The symbols are deliberately employed by Progoff to promote communication between the surface and the 'depths' of the person. They have the same effect when used less formally in individual or group prayer; indeed their effectiveness may be greater when they are used more naturally and spontaneously. These symbols play a very important part in religious experience. In so far as they facilitate communication with 'the depths' they dispose one to let go to God; and they also give expression to the degree of self-surrender which has already been accomplished.

We have considered four means which can be used to dispose one to let go to God: rhythmic prayer, prayer in tongues, listening to God in 'the depths', and the use of basic religious symbols. But there remains another means, one which is generally the most important of all; this is to let go to other people. Self-surrender to God is frequently related closely to an entrusting of oneself to one or more people. In the Charismatic Renewal the group plays an important role in this regard. So we shall devote our final chapter to some remarks about the role of the group.

8. LETTING GO TO THE GROUP

To surrender to God is to trust him, to entrust oneself to him in response to his unconditional love. But as we saw in the previous chapter, at the deep level at which such a letting go takes place there is room only for a single global stance. This will later branch out into an openness to God, to other people, to the world. But at the core, the response to God and to others are effectively one. This is perhaps the deep psychological basis for St John's claim that 'he who does not love his brother whom he has seen, cannot love God whom he has not seen' (1 *John* 4: 20). That statement is equally true if we replace the word 'love' with the word 'trust'.

Let us now take for granted the primal connection between trusting God and trusting others; can we go on from there and see any special role to be played by other people in the particular kind of self-surrender to God needed by the dutiful Christian? The first thing to say is that such a breakthrough can take place without any obvious immediate involvement of others. One thinks for instance of the well-documented experiences of Pascal and of Thérèse of Lisieux. But in a very large number of cases a sudden breakthrough has come while the person was being prayed over by a group. The believer sees in this a speedy answer by God to the fervent prayer of the group. But is there a secondary causality involved? Yes, I think a psychological explanation can be given. It involves two elements. Firstly, there is no doubt that the expectation aroused or focused by the prayer plays an important part in the process of self-surrender. And secondly I would like to argue that there is a real mediation by which letting go to God is effected in and through letting go to the group.

The role of the group

A group of people may have been acquaintances or even friends for years; but if they begin to pray spontaneously together there is generally a remarkable change in their relationship. Individuals become more ready to express their difficulties openly. This evokes the compassion and concern of the others. The friendship deepens. The members are no longer reluctant to express their love and concern for each other. So the group becomes very supportive of all its members, not merely in everyday difficulties but even in the personal religious development of each of them. The growing trust and openness in the group encourages each individual to trust God more fully and surrender more completely to him.

If a member of such a group comes to realise that there is something seriously lacking in his or her experience of Christianity and feels a need to let go more fully and affectively to God, it is natural for the person to turn to the group for spiritual support. And it is only natural that the group should choose some occasion on which to focus their prayer on this individual's need. If the group are accustomed to express concern in a visible and tangible way by praying over individuals at times of special need, then they will find it natural to do so on this occasion also. We have here all the elements that go to make up the ceremony of praying for baptism in the Spirit. And obviously the whole affair is something that should be normal for the group, not some exotic ritual imported from outside.

When people pray over a member of their group in this way the whole atmosphere can be very conducive to a breakthrough in the person's relationship with God. The two key elements in the atmosphere are an intensely prayerful expectation of a breakthrough and a warm sense of openness and mutual trust in the group, inviting the person to let go. In combination, these go a long way towards melting the reserve or inhibitions of the person being prayed for.

Suppose the prayer 'works' there and then—that is, the person experiences a sudden sense of letting go and becomes filled with peace and joy. The whole group will, quite rightly, see in this a yielding to God and an outpouring of his love. The group is not interested in analysing the situation from a psychological point of view. So they scarcely advert to the fact that the self-surrender to God has involved a letting go in front of the group and therefore a certain exposure of the person and a letting go *to* the group.

Afterwards, however, the person who has been prayed for will find that he or she has attained a new kind of intimacy with the rest of the group; and the group as a whole finds itself more closely knit together by the experience. Even if the members do not put it in so many words, they will normally be aware that the self-surrender of the person to God has been mediated in some way through a letting go to the group. This is perfectly normal. In fact it is just a particularly heightened instance of something that has been going on since the group seriously began praying together.

A new world

Letting go to a religious group in this way can have very different meanings, depending on the character of the group. The prayer-group may be a *sect* or part of a sect. In this case it offers to the individual who joins it a set of ultimate beliefs and values. This overall framework becomes for the person the source of order and meaning in life. It gives the person the security of not having to face an unintelligible world.[1] From the point of view of the sociology of knowledge this person has really entered into another world, the world constructed by the religious group he is joining. Is it any wonder then that letting go to a group can be such a dramatic experience? And it is not surprising that the person's whole life-style may change. Many of the person's past activities are now experienced as quite meaningless or valueless.

When the group is part of the Charismatic Renewal the situation is rather different and more complicated. For the Renewal is very careful to remain within the Church, rather than be a sect. This means that the ultimate frame of meaning adopted by such prayer groups is the Christian one. In principle it is shared with millions of other Christians—including those local Christians who do not belong to the prayer-group. But letting go to such a group is a very different kind of thing to, say, joining a sodality or pious association within the Church. It involves a type of self-giving which is far deeper. For though the prayer-group is not a sect from a theological point of view it has many of the characteristics of one from a sociological point of view. *In practice,* then, a prayer-group of this type may provide a new world for many of the individuals who join it. Indeed it is not uncommon to hear such a description being given by people within the group.

It would be easy to conclude from this that the Charismatic Renewal is very much like a sect, despite protestations to the contrary. I think this conclusion is too facile. It fails to take account of the delicate relationship that exists between the group and the wider Church, both at the theological level and at a more practical level.[2] To illustrate this, let us consider two represent-ative types of person who join prayer-groups.

The first type is represented by the person who up to this point has been a nominal or careless Christian. This means that the person has been socialised into what is called the Christian world. Life will have been lived more or less in accord with those general Christian attitudes which are part of the culture of the Western world. But this is not really a Christian world in the proper sense. It is like the dry bones in the vision of Ezekiel. It lacks the breath of life:

> Then he said to me, 'Prophesy . . . and say to the breath, Thus says the Lord God: Come from the four winds, O breath, and breathe upon these slain, that they may live.' So I prophesied as he commanded me, and the breath came into them, and they lived, and stood upon their feet . . . (*Ezek.* 37:9-10).

In this case the breath that comes to bring life is the faith that alone can bring personal subjective meaning into a Christian world. This faith is both a gift of God and a personal act on the part of the one who believes—indeed it is an act which becomes a state. It is mediated to the person in this case through the process of letting go to the group.

The second typical kind of person who joins a prayer group is what we have called the 'dutiful Christian'. We would not want to say that such a person did not have Christian faith prior to letting go. But the faith had not permeated the person's life; it was blocked, particularly in the affective area. So when the breakthrough occurs, whether suddenly or cumulatively, the person has the sensation of entering a new world. It might be more accurate to call it a newly illuminated world. Such a description would echo the accounts of many people who say that it wasn't so much that they learned anything new but that the Christian world and teaching now began to seem real to them for the first time.

Although the universe of meaning adopted by a Charismatic Renewal group is that of Christianity as a whole, the group itself has to have many of the features of a 'subsociety' (in Peter Berger's sense[3]). It has to have its own 'plausibility structures' to maintain the new (or newly illumined) world which its members have entered. To recognise this is to understand the function played by certain practices of the Charismatic Renewal. The most obvious example is of course the practice of praying in tongues. Apart from its religious function, this has a social function, namely, that it identifies the person with the group and sets up a kind of boundary (not to say a barrier) around the group. The Charismatic Renewal has several distinctive practices, e.g. 'prophecy', laying on of hands, prayer for healing or 'deliverance', the lifting up of hands in prayer, certain typical styles for praying, and the giving of testimonies. This all adds up to a very clearly defined group identity.[4] The regular and frequent prayer meetings ensure that the individual's sense of the reality of the Christian world is constantly being renewed.

A minority world

The sociologist looking at all this would have to admit that it is a very effective formula for 'reality maintenance'. Unfortunately, it is not uncommon for sociologists to go on to make explicit or implicit value-judgments on the basis of their unacknowledged prejudices. For instance it is all too easy to slip into the assumption that the sociological explanation somehow shows up the whole process as a kind of brainwashing or manipulation. One could then dismiss the world that it constructs and

E

maintains, without ever bothering to ask about its validity or objectivity. It is important to remember that every 'world' has to have plausibility structures and devices to construct and maintain its experienced reality. What is distinctive about the particular world in question here is not that it is maintained in this way but that it is the world of a 'cognitive minority'. To an increasing extent, committed Christians find themselves living in a minority situation. Inevitably this means that the world of a Christian cannot any longer have the quality of being totally taken for granted. That was possible in the Middle Ages. But now we have a pluralist situation, with different world-views in competition with one another. Inevitably then the devices for world-maintenance are more obvious, especially when the world is that of a minority.

It would seem, then, that committed Christians must, with open eyes and quite aware of what they are doing, join with others who share their faith in maintaining the sense of the reality of their world. This is a necessary community aspect of any kind of faith, deriving from the fact that we are social by nature. This might be done through techniques that approximate to brainwashing; one can see that happening among certain religious or quasi-religious movements of our time. But it need not happen that way. World-maintenance does not have to be manipulative. Nor does it have to be elitist nor a retreat from the real world. On the contrary, the Christian believes that faith opens up deeper dimensions of our world and gives us a truer conception of its nature and purpose. Human freedom is a crucial part of the true Christian world and the means used to maintain that world must at all costs respect this freedom. In the present pluralist situation, and in the light of our deeper appreciation of the sacredness of conscience, it seems to me that leaders of the Charismatic Renewal should make every effort to ensure that members are aware of how their world is maintained. Faith should be conscious and fully free not only in its deep personal roots but even in this social aspect of it.

One sometimes hears warnings that the Charismatic Renewal is in danger of becoming a sect.[5] That this is possible can scarcely be denied. It would be a move in that direction if local group activities were to take priority over local Church activities such as worship with the Christian community. Or if regional or national leaders began to play the role which Church authorities should have. But in my limited experience this has not happened to any very alarming extent. It is true that within the Renewal certain communities have developed, where the members submit themselves to community authorities to a very considerable degree. But the development of religious societies and congregations of all types within the unity of the Catholic Church teaches us that allegiance to a community does not necessarily lessen a person's loyalty to the Church.

Until fairly recently the weekly prayer-meeting was the principal embodiment of the Charismatic Renewal, or even the only one. Now a greater variety is developing: some people are forming into very closely knit communities, while others are introducing 'charismatic' elements into the ordinary liturgical life of the Church (e.g. in 'prayers of the faithful') and into the daily secular life that is shared with people who do not attend a prayer-meeting. This pluriformity is good. And it is particularly important that it should not be only in a prayer-meeting that people have the opportunity to pray together spontaneously and at a deep level.

Participants in the Charismatic Renewal prefer that it should not be called a 'movement'. That is a healthy instinct but there are some practical conclusions which should follow. Perhaps the most important is that no attempt should be made to categorise some people as 'in' the Renewal and others as not 'in' it. One can be 'in' a movement. But a renewal is something less clearly definable; it can be promoted in many different ways and degrees. One helpful way for many people is participation in a prayer-meeting. But that is not the only means by which the individual and the Church can be charismatically renewed.

Insistence on the fact that the aim is renewal of the Church rather than promotion of a movement will help the members of a prayer-group to avoid thinking, feeling, or acting like a sect. They will find themselves promoting a double structure of organisation and authority. On the one hand there is the group's own leadership; and on the other hand there are the structures and authorities of the wider Church. The member will experience a dual sense of belonging. Loyalty to the group may be more immediate. But the ultimate, overriding loyalty will be to the Church.

Surveys indicate that those who participate in charismatic prayer-groups tend to become more loyal to their Church.[6] That is as it should be—provided of course that the loyalty includes an element of constructive criticism. Without that there is little hope of renewal. On the other hand, the Charismatic Renewal does not seek a total dismantlement and re-building. It tries to be charismatic—open to the gifts of the Spirit; and the greatest of these gifts is love. This means that letting go to the group should be not merely a symbol and means of yielding to God, but also a symbol and a means of full loving commitment to the Church.

Conservative?

If people in the Charismatic Renewal pay more attention to their own group than to the Church, they can be accused of being sectarian. But on the other hand if they show increased loyalty to the Church, they find their attitude dismissed as 'a conservative reaction to rapid social and cultural change'.[7] It is no part of my aim in this book to make a thorough assessment of the validity of such a judgment. For my principal concern is not the Charismatic Renewal as such, but the experience which the Renewal calls 'baptism in the Spirit' and which can also be found outside the Renewal. However, I think I should remark in passing that though the accusation has some basis in fact it appears to me to overlook other important aspects of the truth.

It is undoubtedly true that the Charismatic Renewal helps participants to experience their religion at a time when Churches are often felt to have become rather secularised and religious devotion is in short supply. So it involves a return to religion. However, this religion takes a very different form from the old-style devotion. In the way the religious experience is channelled it is not really a return to the past for most of the participants; rather it is felt to be something new. So it seems unwarranted to call it a conservative reaction—unless one assumes that for a secularised person to become religious is automatically a conservative reaction; and such an assumption should be challenged.

In some respects the Charismatic Renewal fosters a break with traditional social and cultural norms. For instance Catholics and Protestants in Northern Ireland are taking a rather radical step by participating together in prayer-meetings. And for the ordinary Christian it involves a considerable degree of liberation from prevailing norms to feel free enough to pray spontaneously with outstretched hands. In these matters the Renewal is anything but conservative. It stands at the opposite pole to traditionalist movements such as that begun by Archbishop Lefebvre. It is opposed by many conservative Church leaders and is supported by leaders like Cardinal Suenens.

On doctrinal and theological issues the Charismatic Renewal tends by and large to be identified with positions that would be called conservative. This is partly the effect of the influence of Pentecostalism, and the fundamentalism which attaches to it. But another and probably more fundamental explanation is that it is a reaction against the very secularist type of theology which became popular some years ago. This theology was so insistent on the autonomy of the world that it found little room for a close personal involvement by God in the details of our lives; or at least that is how it came across at the popular level. No wonder then that it was felt to be quite inadequate by people who were discovering that the Holy Spirit offers a guidance which is not just a general set of rules and a fund of goodwill, or people who were finding that prayers for healing could be answered.

This leads me on to suggest that a theological outlook which seems conservative should perhaps be explained not so much as a conservative clinging to the past but more in terms of a 'spiritual pragmatism'.[8] This means that a position is accepted primarily because it seems to fit in with the religious experience of the participants. To illustrate this let us consider three instances of the kind of outlook that would be typical within the Renewal. In liturgical matters the outlook tends to be rather liberal. In regard to evil spirits the outlook tends to be conservative. In regard to praying in tongues the outlook is not really liberal or conservative but is largely borrowed from a different tradition. What all three have in common is that they provide a basis for the actual religious practices and devotion common in the Renewal. In one sense the theology guides the practice. But in a sense that is perhaps more basic the practice is the source of the theology: 'the law of prayer is the law of belief'.

This quality of spiritual pragmatism gives one grounds for hope that the Charismatic Renewal can find room for a rather more nuanced theology than that which prevails at present. It could become less influenced by fundamentalism. And it could become more open to a conception of God as working through secondary causes. The basic condition for the acceptability of such a theology would be that it should nourish rather than undermine the religious experience of participants. I hope this condition is met by the theology of grace, faith, and baptism in the Spirit which I have outlined in this book.

Search for security

Some of those who consider the Charismatic Renewal conservative are judging it mainly in terms of the social and political attitudes of its participants. Is their judgment soundly based? It is a fact that most of the participants in the Western world have a middle-class background. And it is true that such people seldom desire radical social and political changes. It is even true that some of them link their religious outlook to their social views. But the real issue is whether consciously or even unconsciously the whole spirituality of the Renewal is one that legitimates the social *status quo* and hinders attempts to bring about changes in society.

Marx and Freud showed very effectively that people who are politically oppressed or psychologically immature may use religion as an escape. It may provide them with a sense of security in the face of the troubles and insecurity of their lives. It can be an 'opium of the people' in offering reward in the next life for putting up with injustice here below. But in addition to this popular accusation against religion there is a much more subtle and convincing one. It is that religion tends to give an impression that the existing social order is God-given and therefore unchangeable. This would mean that to become more religious is automatically to become more conservative, less willing to tamper with the given institutions of society and of the Church itself.

Fortunately Peter Berger, who gives perhaps the best expression of this argument against religion, goes on to give an answer to it.[9] Briefly, his view is that religion is frequently used to buttress the existing social order by giving it a sacred character as coming from God. But religion does not necessarily work in this way. In fact it can also provide a basis for the exact opposite approach—a calling into question of all human institutions. If God is understood to be truly transcendent, then the social order can be seen to have no inherent sanctity or immortality. And human authorities can be challenged in the name of God—as was done by the prophets of Israel.

In practice, a heightened religious consciousness may be either a very conservative force or a very radical one. Among strict Pentecostalists the conservative tendency is more common. But there are remarkable examples, especially in the poorer parts of the world, of Pentecostalism being linked with political radicalism.[10] It is still too soon to predict which direction the Charismatic Renewal will take, or whether it will branch in two contrary directions, as Pentecostalism has. Indeed the whole idea of prediction is not really helpful since the direction taken is a very contingent thing, depending largely on the free decisions of influential leaders and of ordinary participants.

Instead of trying to make predictions it seems better to work with conviction and hope to ensure that living faith in God is not subverted in a way that makes of it a blindly conservative force. For this would really be a subversion and distortion of Christian faith. The intrinsic dynamic of the faith is towards a radical questioning of unjust social structures. Believers are called to stand in the tradition of the prophets—comforting the oppressed and challenging the smug. This is because they have discovered a *transcendent* source of order, meaning, and security.

People who are baptised in the Spirit frequently speak of finding in God a profound source of security. That is not a sign of escapism or immaturity; or at least it should not be. Rather it should set these people free from looking for security in the existing social structures (conservatism), or in a political leader (messianism), or in an unprovable theory about history (dialectical materialism), or in wealth, power and pleasure (the common malaise of the Western World). One is rescued from such idols by finding security in the loving hands of the provident Father.

However, the security one finds in God can come to be associated with something in our world. This can occur in various ways, but most commonly through a fundamentalist notion of the commands of God. The result is a legalistic conservatism, a kind of phariseeism, which distorts the whole idea of God. The remedy for such blind religious conservatism is not the elimination of religion; but better religion. That means religion where the object of faith is the transcendent God. Every effort of a prayer-group should then be turned towards helping people to have such an authentic faith. To be baptised in the Spirit in its proper sense is to have that kind of faith. That is why the circumstances in which the group prays for it for one of its members are of the greatest importance.

Excessive pressure

Prayer over a person for baptism in the Spirit is generally a turning-point in the relation of that person to the prayer-group. Willingness to take this step (including the customary weeks of preparation for it) seals his or her commitment and desire to enter the world shared by the other members. So it is particularly important that the freedom of the person be fully respected at this crucial time.

A group who arrange to pray over somebody ought to organise it in a way that ensures that no undue psychological pressure is exerted on the person concerned. Obviously, anything that would lend itself to mass hysteria is to be avoided—particularly the practice of conducting the ceremony for large groups of people together, in something of a revivalist atmosphere. For in such a situation the individual comes under tremendous psychological pressure as a result of seeing others falling down or crying out.[11] There are also some kinds of music and hymns that can be used to generate an emotionally-charged atmosphere to a degree that would interfere with the effective freedom of sensitive or suggestible people.

A more subtle type of pressure can be exerted on people by the way in which the concept of baptism in the Spirit is presented to them. People may be led to believe that without a sudden breakthrough they are lacking the fullness of Christian life. The fact that letting go can in many cases be a gradual and cumulative process may be ignored or played down.[12] Those who have had the more dramatic type of breakthrough may tend to form an elite in-group which others feel pressurised to join.

Furthermore, undue pressure can be put on individuals by an atmosphere that is dominated by an expectation of the wonders of God. Not that there is anything wrong with expecting wonders; in fact the Christian should expect them. But what often happens is that *suddenness* is taken to be the definitive mark or proof of God's intervention. The underlying assumption is that a more gradual letting go to God might be at least partly due to human effort; whereas when there is a sudden break-through it has to be a free, unmerited, direct and wondrous work of God. Such an attitude is a carry-over from Pentecostalism, which in turn inherited it from the older Evangelical spirituality where the suddenness of a conversion was taken as proof that it was 'of grace alone'.[13] It would be rather sad if the Charismatic Renewal were to adopt such a naïve theology just at a time when many in the Evangelical tradition have come to a more nuanced understanding of how God's causality operates.

In general, it seems wiser to avoid making a sharp contrast between God's direct intervention and merely natural causality.[14] Far better to foster that type of faith which sees God's intimate involvement in all that takes place,[15] operating through a tran-scendent causality. If we try to pin down God's intervention to this or that particular occasion, we may be in danger of neglect-ing his presence in *every* happening of our lives. So it is important to cultivate the kind of faith that leaves God free to perform his wonders in many different ways. This has the effect of leaving to individuals the freedom they need to advance along the particular route to which God has called them, rather than have somebody else's pattern imposed on them.

The problem of having to conform to a pattern can be a serious one. In the history of Christianity there are many in-stances where the particular religious experience of a spiritual leader comes to be set up as the definitive pattern to be followed by all disciples. The result is a pressure on all within that tradition to conform to the ideal pattern. It is important for prayer-groups to be aware of this danger. They must be ready to allow for a great variety of patterns of religious growth, instead of expecting everybody to fit the pattern of the sudden breakthrough.[16]

Newcomers

It sometimes happens that people from outside the group are present while prayer for baptism in the Spirit is taking place. For such observers the experience can be rather off-putting or even frightening. I think they realise instinctively that the person being prayed for is being put under some pressure not merely to yield to God but also to let go to the group. And the immediate reaction of an outsider is one of feeling threatened. This sense of threat can turn into a kind of fascination which draws people almost against their wills to ask to be prayed over themselves. In my opinion this is not a healthy situation. For individuals of this kind may later reject the fascination rather violently and become quite hostile to the idea of shared prayer. Or alternatively they may be drawn too suddenly into the whole new world which is presented to them. A more gradual initiation seems more respectful of their freedom. So I think it is better that newcomers should not normally intrude on the more intimate religious experiences of a group such as praying solemnly that an individual be baptised in the Spirit.

Normally, then, a group ought not to pray over somebody for baptism in the Spirit unless that person is well known to them and has been praying with them for some time. It occasionally happens that somebody drops in on a prayer meeting and wants to be prayed over immediately for baptism in the Spirit. Such people may say, 'I might as well give it a try; it cannot do me any harm and it might help me.' To agree to such a request does do harm, at times at least. It can give the impression that this is some powerful type of ritual which may or may not work. This mythologises the whole thing. And it contributes to a polarisation of people for or against baptism in the Spirit. In effect it gives the Charismatic Renewal the aura of a sect with a sudden baptism in the Spirit as its initiation rite.

When to ask

It requires considerable spiritual sensitivity for an individual to know when to ask to be prayed over for baptism in the Spirit. The difficulty would not be so great if the person and the praying group accepted and acted on the view that a gradual and cumulative breakthrough is just as good as a sudden and dramatic one. But in practice a good deal of the spirituality of prayer-groups tends to centre around baptism in the Spirit envisaged as a sudden letting go. This leaves the individual with the problem of knowing whether it is wise to undergo this kind of ceremony— that is, whether it would fit in with the pattern of this person's religious experience; and if so, when would be the right time for it.

People in this situation need to discern the pattern of their spiritual development. A wise spiritual director is an almost indispensable help in this task. And obviously such spiritual directors need to be aware not only of the spiritual state of the person but also of what is involved in being baptised in the Spirit. Somebody with an inadequate understanding of what it means is liable to be naïvely against it. This shows once again the importance of relating Pentecostal-type spirituality to the traditional spiritualities of the historic Churches.

Suppose a careful process of spiritual discernment convinces someone that he or she is being led closer to God in a gradual and cumulative way. He or she has not become aware of any distinct 'block' which obstructs this progress. There are of course occasional lapses and general weakness; but there is no settled attitude of unyielding resistance. In these circumstances there is a good argument for *not* undergoing a formal ceremony of being prayed over for baptism in the Spirit. This is because this formal prayer, as usually understood and carried out at present, seems to aim primarily at a sudden breakthrough rather than the cumulative one which is the road to God of the person we are considering. So it seems more respectful both to God (who has chosen this way in this instance) and to the person's own spiritual situation, not to look for a sudden type of letting go. Of course a more informal type of prayer by the group for the person is always a help. And there is no reason why the group should not occasionally pray over the person for greater openness to God and to others.

Dryness

In discerning whether or when to undergo the formal cere-mony of being prayed over, the person should not judge simply in terms of the presence or absence of feelings of well-being or a vivid sense of the presence of God. The real test is whether one is yielding to God, in mind and heart. Spiritual feelings help one to discern whether or not this is happening. But we need some rules for discernment such as those proposed by Ignatius Loyola. It would be far too naïve simply to correlate self-surrender with consolation and to assume that dryness or sadness necessarily involve a failure to let go to God.[17] Anybody who studies the writings of the spiritual masters cannot doubt that God does at times lead us into the desert, teaching us to trust him in dryness. He allows us to undergo deep spiritual suffering, as Christ did:

> In the days of his flesh, Jesus offered up prayers and supplica-tions, with loud cries and tears, to him who was able to save him from death . . . Although he was a Son, he learned obedi-ence through what he suffered . . . (*Heb.* 5 : 7-8).

Suppose somebody has truly yielded to God, not only by a deliberate choice but also in a way that involves the heart—that is, the centre of affectivity. Such a person may be led by God through a process of purification where no obvious consolation can be felt. In such a situation, to ask to be prayed over for baptism in the Spirit would, I think, indicate a failure either to understand or to accept one's spiritual state. But if, on the other hand, it becomes clear that the real problem is a failure to let go one's affectivity to God, then it could be very helpful to have some close friends carry out the ceremony of praying over one.

Some deeply spiritual people live for years on end in a kind of spiritual desert. Perhaps the most difficult issue of discern-ment is to know whether such aridity is a trial from God or whether it stems from a failure to let go one's heart to God. It is important to note that these two possibilities are not mutually exclusive. God's causality is transcendent, making use of a variety of secondary causes. So a state of aridity which is rightly considered a trial willed by God, may at the same time be explicable in psychological terms as due to an inability to let go in total trust to God. If this is found to be the situation, there is a good case for being formally prayed over for baptism in the Spirit.

The crucial point in such a case is that the person involved is not looking primarily for a feeling of joy or release, but for deep self-surrender to God. If such a letting go does take place it will in fact involve a more profound spiritual freedom and peace. But this will not eliminate the possibility of dryness or real spiritual suffering.[18] However, underlying the dryness there will remain a thirst for God, a faith-conviction of his presence. John of the Cross conveys something of the situation in the following lines:

> For I know well the spring that
>   flows and runs,
>   Although it is night . . .

> Its clarity is never darkened,
> And I know that every light has
>   come from it
>   Although it is night.[19]

In the suffering and darkness there remains a deeper half-submerged joy—'I rejoice in my sufferings' (*Col.* 1:24). Behind even the sense of dereliction felt by Christ on the cross was his firm hope in his Father. This is indicated by his choice of Psalm 22. It begins, 'My God, my God, why hast thou forsaken me?' (*Matt.* 27:46). But it goes on later, 'he has not hid his face . . . but has heard . . .' (*Ps.* 22:24).

A risk

We have seen that letting go to a group can mediate a person's yielding to God. But now we must note that this process can go wrong. The psychological breakthrough which takes place may be far more successful as a yielding to the group than as a surrender to God. There may be a convulsive sense of letting go, with a consequent feeling of freedom, security and peace. But that may happen in a way that does not carry the person beyond the group to God.

This is a serious religious failure. It means that the group is allowed to take the central role which should be God's. In this case yielding to the group has become the *goal* of the ceremony rather than being a symbol of the person's surrender to God. Acceptance by the group has become an end rather than a means. The group, rather than God, has become the source of security and freedom.

All this can take place in varying degrees. It is not an all-or-nothing affair. If it does happen, the fault may lie in the group or in the individual. It is far less likely to happen where the group has been careful not to act like a sect. For the group that is seen, and sees itself, as a means of facilitating full involvement in the life of the Church, can more easily facilitate a person's full surrender to God himself.

If it should happen to any considerable degree that the person has let go to the group rather than to God, the results can be very damaging, not only religiously but also morally. The person will be emotionally dependent on the group. At best this leads to immaturity and a failure to develop in conscience and character. At worst it could lead to gross abuses, where a kind of psychological slavery takes place.

It is well to be aware, then, that when there is question of letting go to a group, powerful forces are being handled and certain risks are being taken. Various cults of recent times give ample proof of the extent to which the process can be abused. Such abuses serve as a warning that anybody who wishes to let go to a group must make a careful choice of time, place and people.

But abuses should not be presented as an argument against ever letting go to others. For the ability to commit ourselves in total trust to others is one of our greatest human gifts. It is doubtful to what extent human fulfilment is possible at all if one is never prepared to take the risk of letting go to another person or a group. The link between this and self-surrender to God is very close.

God may or may not choose to use others to mediate our letting go to him in a sudden and dramatic way. But whether or not our yielding to God takes the form of a sudden breakthrough, and whether or not others play an obvious instrumental role in it, we cannot be open to God if we refuse to be open to others. If we insist on wearing a mask all the time before others, how can we stand naked and helpless before God? We have to be prepared to let others see us weak and broken if we are to be saved from the attitude of self-sufficiency which masks a deep anxiety. We have to be willing to admit, even before others, the futility of our own efforts, if we want to be 'saved by grace through faith' (*Eph.* 2:8). For God's power finds its point of insertion when we acknowledge our weakness (2 *Cor.* 11:30; 1 *Cor.* 1:27). We must suffer the death of letting go the life *we* construct and control if we are to bear fruit (cf. *John* 12:24). Only then can God fulfil his promise:

> I shall give you a new heart, and put a new spirit in you;
> I shall remove the heart of stone from your bodies
> and give you a heart of flesh instead. (*Ezek.* 36:26).

Conclusion

There are different ways in which faith can be experienced. For some people a vivid sense of the Father's care seems quite normal; and Christ and the Spirit are part of the fabric of their lives. Others have what Karl Rahner would call a 'wintertime' experience of faith; the life of faith is largely under the surface; it does not flower into any vivid awareness of God. This image of a 'wintertime' type of faith is helpful. But it can be misused. Many people simply assume that their rather barren experience of faith is due to their temperament and to the kind of world we have today. And they don't really want to change. They are content to live in this winter without hoping seriously that they will ever in this life experience the new life of spring.

Such an attitude should be challenged. We may ask *why* it is that some people live more or less permanently in the wintertime situation while in others faith flowers abundantly. Human explanations can go some way towards providing an answer, though of course an element of mystery remains. People are quite right in their assumption that it is largely a combination of personal temperament and the environment we live in today. But they are wrong in assuming that these cannot be changed. The temperament that is practically closed to a warm religious experience is largely the product of a life-history of anxiety and hurt. But hurts can be healed and anxiety can be swept away by an experience of being totally loved and accepted. Similarly, it is quite true that the harsh wind of a secularist world makes it difficult for faith to blossom. There is very little in the environment of the world today that would give one a vivid sense that this world is loved by the Father, redeemed by Christ, and illumined by the Holy Spirit. But even the environment we live in is not entirely beyond our control. The Christian is committed to the transformation of the world. An important step in the process is the construction of a local environment which would be an image and kind of sacrament of what the world could be.

A group of committed Christians can form a subsociety with a climate that favours the blossoming of faith and an environment in which God's care and involvement seem real and relevant to daily life. This environment helps people to let go to God at a deep affective level. It is a healing experience. It can liberate people from chronic anxiety. It can open them up in a new way to the living and loving God who says:

> Arise, my love, my fair one,
>   and come away;
> for lo, the Winter is past,
>   the rain is over and gone.
> The flowers appear on the earth,
>   the time of singing has come.
>   (*Song of Songs* 2 : 10-12).

NOTES

Introduction
(pp. 1-5)
1. Until recently, Pentecostalism was generally thought of as a rather unusual form of evangelical Protestantism. This may be true from a historical point of view. But it is now widely accepted that from a theological and sociological point of view the Pentecostal Churches should be regarded as a distinct tradition within Christianity.

2. Cf. Peter Hocken's remarks in his excellent contribution to *New Heaven? New Earth?: An Encounter with Pentecostalism*, London: Darton, Longman & Todd 1976, 38: 'The greater openness of the Catholic tradition towards nature and creation can ground a different and more flexible understanding of Pentecostalism's potential.'

3. See for instance, Eduardo F. Pironio, 'Evangelizacion y liberacion' in *Evangelizzazione e Culture (Atti del Congresso Internazionale Scientifico di Missiologia, Roma 5-12 Ottobre 1975)*, Rome: Pontificia Università Urbaniana 1976, vol. II, 494-513. Cf. the remark of John Orme Mills in his contribution to *New Heaven? New Earth?* (see note 2 above), 117: 'It is fashionable to contrast Latin America's Christian freedom fighters and its "charismatics" and overlook how much they have in common.' See also the references in note 10 of chapter 8 below.

4. Cf. the helpful distinction made by Jean Mouroux between three types of religious experience: an *empirical* type (emotions), an *experimental* type (states reached by the use of techniques like concentration), and an *experiential* type (fully personal) which 'strives to be total . . . attains and puts in their proper order all the levels of human nature . . .'—'Religious Experience', *Sacramentum Mundi*, vol. V, London: Burns & Oates 1970, 292.

Chapter 1
MEETING THE GIVER IN THE GIFTS
(pp. 9-20)

1. E.g. J. P. Mackey, *The Problem of Religious Faith,* Dublin: Helicon 1972, 20: 'Religious faith . . . is one of the approaches of the human mind to reality, or one of the points of access that link reality to the human organism and provide for reaction between them.'

2. Cf. below, chapter 8, 134-5 and chapter 3, 150.

3. George A. Aschenbrenner, 'Consciousness Examen' in *Review for Religious* 31 (1972), 14.

4. Cf. the remark of John Hyde in his very perceptive assessment of J. P. Mackey's *Life and Grace,* Dublin: Gill 1966. Having noted that for Mackey the meaning of 'grace' is the fellowship of God with man, Hyde says: 'Now if I were looking for an account of "grace" in the author's sense, I would not go to a textbook of dogmatic theology at all, but to works on prayer or spiritual life or something else. I think that in fact the tradition has always been faithfully handed on, and very much cherished and valued and cultivated. The text-books suppose that the student of theology has already received it, and they deal with subsidiary questions which arise from it. . . . Whether this is pedagogically the best situation for modern times is another matter.'—*The Furrow* 18 (August 1967), 482. I would add that the problem is not merely pedagogical; the separation led to an impoverishment in both the streams into which it split—the systematic and the ascetical.

Chapter 2
A THEOLOGICAL-SPIRITUAL JOURNEY
(pp. 21-32)

1. E.g. G. Van Noort, *Tractatus de Gratia Christi* (4th ed.—J. P. Verhaar), Hilversum: Paulus Brand 1960, 154: '. . . ipsa gratia secundum se, quum supernaturalis sit, conscientiam superat . . .'; L. Billot, *De Gratia Christi,* Prati: Giachetti 1912, 207; J. Van der Meersch, 'Grâce' in *DTC,* VI, 1616ff.

2. J. Van der Meersch, *art.cit.,* 1624: '. . . nous ne pourrons jamais savoir avec certitude parfait que cet acte est *surnaturel,* puisque . . . nous ne pouvons en percevoir immédiatement la sur-naturalité . . .'

3. *Ibid.,* 1617f.

4. M. J. Scheeben, *Nature and Grace* (Eng. trs. by C. Vollert), St Louis: Herder 1954, 233.

5. Especially the following three articles: 'Concerning the Relation-ship between Nature and Grace' and 'Some Implications of the

Scholastic Concept of Uncreated Grace' in *Theological Investigations,* vol. I, London: Darton, Longman and Todd 1961, 297-317 and 319-46; 'Nature and Grace' 3-43 in *Nature and Grace,* London: Sheed and Ward 1963. Rahner later summed up his position, in the entry under the title 'Grace: Systematic' in *Sacramentum Mundi,* vol. II, 415-22.

6. Published later in English in *Theological Investigations,* vol. III, London: Darton, Longman and Todd 1967, 86-90.

7. London: Sheed and Ward 1955, 274ff.

8. London: Chapman 1966 and 1967.

9. *The Transformation of Man,* 242-3.

10. In Bernard Lonergan, *Grace and Freedom: Operative Grace in the Thought of St Thomas Aquinas,* London: Darton, Longman and Todd 1971; original articles published in 1941-2.

11. I have in mind the work of Peter Berger and Thomas Luckmann; see below, note 1 to chapter 8.

12. The approach I have found most helpful is that of Bernard Lonergan, *Method in Theology,* London: Darton, Longman and Todd 1972.

13. Louis J. Puhl (translator), *The Spiritual Exercises of St Ignatius: Based on Studies in the Language of the Autograph,* Chicago: Loyola University Press 1951.

14. *Spiritual Life* 21 (Spring 1975), 11-12.

15. 'The Thorn and the Rose' in *Spiritual Life* 22 (Summer 1976), 86-95.

16. *Ibid.,* 90.

17. Søren Kierkegaard, *The Concept of Dread* (Eng. trs. by Walter Lowrie), Princeton: Princeton University Press, 2nd ed. 1957, 142-5.

18. 'The Thorn and the Rose', 92.

19. Kierkegaard, *op. cit.* 144. Karl Rahner gives a list of rather similar types of experiences in his article 'Faith, I' in *Sacramentum Mundi,* vol. II, 312: '. . . indescribable joy, unconditional personal love, unconditional obedience to conscience, the experience of loving union with the universe, the experience of the irretrievable vulnerability of one's own existence beyond one's own control . . .'. A more extensive treatment of such experiences is given by the Brazilian theologian Leonardo Boff in his book *A Graça Libertadora no Mundo,* Petropolis: Vozes 1976, 114-28. His list includes the sense of gratuitousness in life, love, success, art, festivity, joy, sorrow, and in the encounter with others. Perhaps the most outstanding instance he gives is that of an answer

to prayer for what would have been thought impossible: 'o impossível concreto (não metafísico) se tornou possível' (p. 120).

20. E.g. Langdon Gilkey *Naming the Whirlwind: The Renewal of God-Language*, Indianapolis: Bobbs-Merrill 1969.

21. Cf. the second of Rahner's articles mentioned in note 5 above; also his remarks in *Sacramentum Mundi*, vol. II, 418.

22. See, for instance, the difficulty Rahner has in trying to distinguish his own conception of 'habitual' and 'actual' grace from the Scholastic conceptions, in, 'Über die Heilsbedeutung der nichtchristlichen Religionen' in *Evangelizzazione e Culture* (note 2 to Introduction, above), vol. I, 298-9.

Chapter 3

BAPTISM IN THE SPIRIT AS A RELIGIOUS EXPERIENCE (pp. 35-54)

1. E.g. S. De Sanctis, *Religious Conversion: a Bio-psychological Study*, London 1927; William James, *The Varieties of Religious Experience*, New York 1902; W. P. Patterson, *Conversion*, London 1939; W. Sargant, *Battle for the Mind*, London 1957; E. D. Starbuck, *The Psychology of Religion*, London 1899; G. Swarts, *Salut par la foi et conversion brusque*, Paris 1931; W. B. Thomas, *The Psychology of Conversion*, London 1935; R. Thouless, *The Psychology of Religion*, 1923 (new edition Cambridge 1961); A. C. Underwood, *Conversion: Christian and Non-Christian*, London 1925.

2. Cf. the remarks of Peter Hocken in *New Heaven? New Earth?* (note 1 to Introduction, above) 36-9 under the heading, 'The Challenge to Pentecostal Self-understanding'.

3. For Wesley's first interpretation see, for instance, *The Journal of the Rev. John Wesley, A.M.* (standard ed. by Curnock), London 1909-16, vol. I, 454-7, 471-2 and 475-6. For later re-interpretation see the footnotes which he added later to his account of his experience—*ibid.* 423-4. See also *The Letters of the Rev. John Wesley, A.M.* (standard ed. by Telford), London 1931, vol. II, 108.

4. See Edward D. O'Connor, *The Pentecostal Movement in the Catholic Church*, Notre Dame: Ave Maria 1971, 1973, 267-79, for a discussion of the reasons why religious experience is considered suspect, despite the importance given to it in Scripture and tradition.

5. Patrick Kavanagh, *Collected Poems*, London: Martin Brian and O'Keefe 1972, 150.

6. *Ibid.*, 3.

Chapter 4
BAPTISM IN THE SPIRIT: THE PENTECOSTAL HERITAGE
(pp. 55-68)

1. Cf. Kilian McDonnell, *Catholic Pentecostalism: Problems in Evaluation*, Pecos: Dove 1970, 14-15; *Theological and Pastoral Orientations on the Catholic Charismatic Renewal* (prepared at Malines Seminar), Notre Dame: The Communications Centre 1974, 28.

2. *Theological and Pastoral Orientations* (note 1, above), 61-2; cf. Cardinal L. J. Suenens, *A New Pentecost?*, London: Darton, Longman and Todd 1975.

3. See, for instance, *The Standard Sermons of John Wesley* (edited by Sugden), London, vol. II, 4th ed. 1956, Sermon 50; also Wesley's *Letters* (note 3 to chapter 3 above), vol. IV, 97, 100; vol. VI, 287; vol. VII, 98.

4. For the historical background to classical Pentecostalism and its early history, see Vinson Synan, *The Holiness-Pentecostal Movement in the United States*, Grand Rapids: Eerdmans 1971; for a brief summary see chapter 1 of the same author's *Charismatic Bridges*, Ann Arbor: Word of Life 1974.

5. See chapter 5, below.

6. The same point is made in a slightly different way in *Theological and Pastoral Orientations* (note 1, above), 23.

7. See chapter 8, below.

8. *The Life in the Spirit Seminars: Team Manual*, Notre Dame: Charismatic Renewal Services, 3rd ed. 1973.

Chapter 5
WHAT'S IN A NAME?
(pp. 71-82)

1. Cf. Stephen B. Clark, *Baptized in the Spirit*, Pecos: Dove 1970, 49: 'Probably, the best reason for using it is historical: this is the term by which most people talk about it today.'

2. Simon Tugwell in, *Did You Receive the Spirit?*, London: Darton, Longman and Todd 1972, 91 and 117, maintains that we should not use the term 'baptism in the Spirit'; he proposes instead, for theological purposes, two terms borrowed from the Christian East—'the discovery of the Spirit' and 'manifestation of baptism'. For a discussion of Tugwell's position see chapter 6, below.

3. A basic source here is the article in Kittel *TWNT* (English ed.), vol. I, 529-46. See also, James D. G. Dunn, *Baptism in the Holy Spirit*, London: SCM 1970; George F. Montague, 'Baptism in the Spirit and Speaking in Tongues: a Biblical Approach' in *Theology Digest* 21 (1973), 342-60; Francis A. Sullivan, ' "Baptism in the Holy Spirit": a Catholic Interpretation of the Pentecostal Experience' in *Gregorianum* 55 (1974), 54-61; Herbert Schneider, 'Baptism in the Holy Spirit in the New Testament' in, Kilian McDonnell (ed.), *The Holy Spirit and Power: The Catholic Charismatic Renewal*, Garden City: Doubleday 1975, 35-55.

4. Dunn, *op. cit.* 54.

5. *Ibid.*, 170, 226.

Chapter 6
THE SACRAMENT OF BAPTISM
(pp. 83-98)

1. E.g. Robert Wild in *Enthusiasm in the Spirit*, Notre Dame: Ave Maria 1975, 64-5, sees the term as a piece of 'theological baggage' which he would like to see dropped; but he adds that it makes people take notice of a neglected aspect of Christian initiation. The Scripture scholar George F. Montague in *art. cit.* (note 3 to chapter 5, above), 348, maintains that the term describes the basic Christian initiation and therefore to apply it to a later experience of awakening in the baptised Christian 'is bound to cause confusion'; so he would prefer to speak of a re-kindling of the gift of God given already. Another leading Scripture scholar, Wilfrid Harrington, writes as follows: ' "Baptism in the Spirit" . . . is a thoroughly biblical phrase, yes—but only if taken in its New Testament meaning. Since it has taken on another, quite different meaning, it is likely to confuse and mislead if it is used in a context of neo-pentecostalism. Yet that other meaning serves as a reminder of the real importance of the Spirit.'—'Spirit of the Living God, III' in *Doctrine and Life* 28 (September 1977), 16.

2. The Malines Document is careful to speak about 'sacramental initiation' rather than just the rite of baptism: see *Theological and Pastoral Orientations* (note 1 to chapter 4, above), 15ff.

3. Stephen B. Clark, in a booklet entitled *Confirmation and the Baptism of the Holy Spirit*, Pecos: Dove 1969, makes some interesting suggestions about how 'baptism in the Spirit' might coincide in time with the reception of the sacrament of Confirma-

tion. But in the present confused state of theology in regard to Confirmation there seems to be little point in trying to establish a theological link between 'baptism in the Spirit' and Confirmation *rather than* baptism, as Clark seems to do in this booklet, though not in his later writings. The best approach is to relate it to the whole rite of initiation, *including* Confirmation.

4. This comparison of marriage and baptism will carry much less force for those Christians who do not accept that marriage is a sacrament. Nevertheless, within the wider theological conception of the Church as sacrament, marriage between Christians can be accepted by Protestants as having a certain sacramental quality; and this suffices to sustain the comparison.

5. On this question of 'expectations' see *Theological and Pastoral Orientations* (note 1 to chapter 4, above), 18-19; also 'The Theological Basis of the Catholic Charismatic Renewal' (document prepared at the Grottaferrata Seminar), Rome (multi-copied: 1973), 4; see also the interesting comparison between 'charismatic' and 'traditional Catholic' types of spirituality, made by Stephen B. Clark in *Baptized in the Spirit* (note 1 to chapter 5, above), 67-70.

6. Cf. Sullivan, *art. cit.* (note 3 to chapter 5, above), 52; J. Massingberd Ford, *The Pentecostal Experience*, New York: Paulist 1970, 24 and 51; Stephen B. Clark, *Baptized in the Spirit* (note 1 to chapter 5, above), 48 and 63; 'Theological Basis' (note 5, above), 6. But note the carefully open and pluralist approach adopted in *The Life in the Spirit Seminars: Team Manual* (note 8 to chapter 4, above), 122f.

7. Cf. Sullivan, *art. cit.* 66.

8. E.g. *Theological and Pastoral Orientations* (note 1 to chapter 4, above), 30-1; 'Theological Basis' (note 5, above), 6; Tugwell, *Did You Receive the Spirit?* (note 2 to chapter 5, above), 29 and 59.

9. See above, chapter 3, 48-9.

10. London: Darton, Longman and Todd 1977. The French original was published in 1975.

11. *Ibid.*, 38.

12. *Ibid.*, 44.

13. *Ibid.*, 40, 46.

14. *Ibid.*, 42.

15. *Ibid.*, 44.

16. *Ibid.*, 41.

17. *Ibid.*, 47; cf. *ibid.*, 35.

18. *Pentecostalism: A Theological Viewpoint,* New York: Paulist 1971, 176-7.
19. *Charism and Sacrament: A Theology of Christian Conversion,* London: SPCK 1977, 150.
20. *Ibid.*
21. Tugwell, *Did You Receive the Spirit?* (note 2 to chapter 5, above), 93.
22. *Ibid.,* 92.
23. Sullivan, *art. cit.* (note 3 to chapter 5, above), 60-1.
24. *Ibid.,* 66.
25. *Ibid.,* 65.
26. Laurentin, *Catholic Pentecostalism* (note 10, above), 45, in his assessment of Sullivan's view, makes much the same point.

Chapter 7
LETTING GO TO GOD
(pp. 101-18)

1. George T. Montague, *Riding the Wind: Learning the Ways of the Spirit,* Ann Arbor: Word of Life 1974, 15.
2. J. Rodman Williams, *The Era of the Spirit,* Plainfield: Logos International 1971, 61-2.
3. There is some similarity between the categories I shall propose and those considered by Stephen B. Clark in, *Baptized in the Spirit* (note 1 to chapter 5, above), 72-4.
4. William James, *The Varieties of Religious Experience* (note 1 to chapter 3, above). James seems to have been influenced by Starbuck who, shortly before James wrote, had made a thorough study of adolescent conversion, concluding that it is a normal part of the process of growing up. See his *The Psychology of Religion* (note 1 to chapter 3, above), 146, 354.
5. Cf. above, chapter 3, 46-7.
6. Cf. Stephen B. Clark, *Baptized in the Spirit* (note 1 to chapter 5, above), 25: Tongues 'allows us to yield to the Spirit'.
7. Cf. Donald L. Gelpi, *Pentecostal Piety,* New York: Paulist 1972, 95.
8. Karl Rahner makes a rather similar point in *Christian at the Crossroads,* London: Burns & Oates 1975, 1977, 63. See also René Laurentin, *Catholic Pentecostalism* (note 10 to chapter 6, above), 157-8: '. . . the Spirit himself is One whom we cannot capture with our objectivising concepts . . .' 'To the extent that a man abandons himself to the action of the Spirit, everything in man proceeds both from the Spirit and from man's own free choice.'

9. The meaning of the text is disputed: it is not clear whether the source of the water is the one who believes in Christ or Christ himself. See Raymond Brown, *The Gospel according to John i-xii*, London: Chapman 1971, 320-4. It may be of interest to recall that this text was used by Agnes Ozman to describe her 'baptism in the Spirit' in 1901—an event which is commonly cited as the beginning of Pentecostalism. See, for instance, Edward D. O'Connor, *The Pentecostal Movement in the Catholic Church*, Notre Dame: Ave Maria 1971, 22.

10. Ira Progoff, *The Symbolic and the Real*, New York: McGraw-Hill Paperbacks 1973, 36. The book was first published in 1963.

11. *Ibid.*, xv. This new introduction was written in 1973.

12. *Ibid.*, 33.

13. *Ibid.*, 35.

14. *Ibid.*, 142-3.

15. *Ibid.*, 145.

16. *Ibid.*, 36.

17. *Ibid.*, 73ff.

18. *Ibid.*, 145.

19. *Ibid.*, 166.

20. See, for instance, the example given by Progoff, *ibid.*, 195.

21. Cf. *ibid.*, 142-3.

22. Agnes Sanford in *The Healing Gifts of the Spirit*, Philadelphia and New York: Lippincott 1966, 51, remarks that behind other causes of depression there is one sure universal cause, namely, that the 'inner light', which is the focus and centre that illumines our being, has gone out.

23. Cf. above, chapter 2, 22.

24. Cf. above, chapter 1, 13.

25. Cf. above, chapter 3, 38-9.

26. *Collected Poems* (note 5 to chapter 3, above), 4. For an interesting but different approach to the question of various kinds of conversion see Donald L. Gelpi, *Charism and Sacrament* (note 19 to chapter 6, above), 17-25. Gelpi stresses the decision aspect of conversion—e.g. '. . . all conversion, religious conversion included, is the decision to turn from irresponsible to responsible behaviour in some area of one's experiential development.' (p. 18). He seems to me to take just one aspect of *moral* conversion as the basic model for understanding different kinds of conversion.

27. *Ibid.*, 149.

28. Eric Voegelin, *Plato and Aristotle* (vol. III of *Order and History*), Baton Rouge: Louisiana State University Press 1957, 192.

29. *Ibid.*, 187; cf. *ibid.*, 62: 'forces of life' are there to help the soul in its apparently hopeless situation; cf. *ibid.*, 84.

30. Cf. above, chapter 1, 12-13, cf. chapter 2, 29.

31. Cf. Henry Duméry, *The Problem of God in Philosophy of Religion*, Northwestern University Press 1964, 27.

32. Cf. Voegelin, *Plato and Aristotle* (note 28, above), 187 and 193-4.

33. For a helpful account, written from within the Thomistic tradition, of how a positive response to a natural instinct can in fact be a genuine act of supernatural faith, see Max Seckler, *Instinkt und Glaubenswille bei Thomas von Aquin*, Mainz 1961.

34. Cf. above, chapter 1, 13.

35. Fynn, *Mister God, This is Anna,* London: Collins Fount Paperbacks 1977, 62. In fact some readers may find that the basic insights about God and religion which I am trying to convey can best be got by reflecting on some other 'lights' of Anna's— e.g. 'Mister God goes right through my middle' (*ibid.*, 62); 'Mister God can love you right inside' (*ibid.*, 41); God is the word that bears the weight of all the other words (*ibid.*, 70).

36. Cf. above, chapter 3, 48-9.

37. For a simple and helpful account of this type of prayer see Abhishiktananda, *Prayer*, London: SPCK 1975, 51-63. For a scientific account of the effects of rhythmic prayer see William Johnston, *Silent Music: The Science of Meditation*, Glasgow: Collins Fontana 1976.

38. See, for instance, Donald L. Gelpi, *Pentecostalism: A Theological Viewpoint* (note 18 to chapter 6, above), 186-91. For a simple introduction to the Ignatian approach to discernment see John C. Haughey, *The Conspiracy of God: The Holy Spirit in Us*, Garden City: Doubleday Image 1976, 105-20. For a rather more detailed treatment see Ladislaus Orsy, *Open to the Spirit*, Denville N. J.: Dimension Books.

39. Progoff, *The Symbolic and the Real* (note 10 above), 113-68.

40. Progoff (*ibid.*, 197) gives an instance of 'tongues' in a person who was not a Christian. For his psychological explanation of the prophetic experience see *ibid.*, 217f.

41. Sanford, *The Healing Gifts of the Spirit* (note 22 above), 113.

42. *Ibid.*, 189.

43. Ira Progoff, *Three Cycles of Process Meditation: 1. The Well and the Cathedral; 2. The Star/Cross; 3. The White-robed Monk*, New York: Dialogue House Library 1971, 1972.

Chapter 8
LETTING GO TO THE GROUP
(pp. 119-38)

1. See Peter Berger and Thomas Luckham, *The Social Construction of Reality: A Treatise in the Sociology of Knowledge,*
   Harmondsworth: Penguin 1972 (originally published in 1966)
   especially 115-20; see also Peter Berger, *The Sacred Canopy:
   Elements of a Sociological Theory of Religion,* Garden City
   N.J.: Anchor 1969, chapters 1 and 2. This book was first published by Doubleday in 1967; a British edition is published under
   the title *The Social Reality of Religion,* Harmondsworth:
   Penguin 1973.

2. It should be noted that the relationship between Church and
   group which I am considering here is the usual one where the
   prayer-group is a minority group within the local Christian
   community. Recently, however, a different approach to Church
   organisation has evolved, especially in parts of Latin America,
   Africa and Asia: the basic Christian community has become the
   local unit of the Church itself. In some places these basic communities may themselves be charismatic prayer-groups. In such
   cases the relationship between the group and the Church is greatly
   simplified; it becomes simply that existing between the local
   community and the wider Church.

3. Berger, *The Sacred Canopy* (note 1, above), 49.

4. Cf. the interesting treatment of 'shared consciousness' in Donald
   L. Gelpi, *Charism and Sacrament* (note 19 of chapter 6, above),
   101-4.

5. E.g. J. Massingberd Ford, 'American Catholic Pentecostalism'
   in *The Furrow* 26 (1975), 199-210. But note that she is speaking
   only of one of the two strands which she detects in the USA.

6. E.g. J. Kerkhofs (ed.), *Catholic Pentecostals Now,* Canfield,
   Ohio: Alba Books 1977, 24. (This book is the material of the
   Pro Mundi Vita Bulletin no. 60, 1976.)

7. James T. Richardson and M. T. Vincent Reidy, 'Neopente-
   costalism in Ireland: A Comparison with the American Experience' in *Social Studies: Irish Journal of Sociology* 5 (Winter
   1976-7), 259; cf. Kerkhofs, *op. cit.* (note 6 above), 51.

8. I borrow this phrase from Peter Hocken who considers that
   'spiritual pragmatism' is a characteristic quality of Pentecostalism.
   See *New Heaven? New Earth?* (note 2 to introduction above), 35.

9. *The Sacred Canopy* (note 1 above). On pp. 87-95 he shows how
   religion can be used to give a sacral quality to social institutions;

the argument derives ultimately from Feuerbach and was used also by Marx. On pp. 96-101 Berger indicates how religion can relativise human institutions.

10. See Walter J. Hollenweger, *Pentecost between Black and White: Five Case Studies on Pentecost and Politics,* Belfast: Christian Journals Ltd, 1974, where there are descriptions of Pentecostal movements which 'function more or less as religious and revolutionary catalysts of transformation in society' (p. 10). Cf. Peter Kami (ed.), *Pentecost and Politics: The Charismatic Church of the World's Poor,* Wick, Bristol: SCM Publications 1976. This booklet documents several instances of Pentecostalist Churches taking a politically radical stance—see especially pp. 2, 14-15, 17-18, 24.

11. Cf. Francis MacNutt, *The Power to Heal,* Notre Dame: Ave Maria 1977, 210: 'I now feel uncomfortable in those meetings where people are falling over, much like pins in a bowling alley, and then are quickly gotten to their feet, so the next person can come up . . .'; cf. *ibid.,* 219: 'I have to admit that when I have been praying and several people, one after the other, have fallen, and then one doesn't go down, I begin to wonder to myself, "Why doesn't this person go down?" It is so easy to judge, to strive for effect! . . . I need to pray to free myself (and everyone else) from any kind of spiritual striving . . . I think it quite possible that some ministers of healing are dealing more in human psychological powers than in the power of the Spirit.'

12. Cf. above, chapter 3, 53, and chapter 4, 59-61.

13. Cf. above, chapter 4, 59 and 64.

14. Cf. Peter Hocken, *New Heaven? New Earth?* (note 2 to Introduction, above), 36: 'The work of the Holy Spirit is . . . understood in terms of miraculous intervention, so promoting an "all or nothing" view of authenticity.' For an instance of a contrast between God's 'direct' intervention and merely natural causality see Edward D. O'Connor, *Pentecost in the Modern World,* Notre Dame: Ave Maria 1972, 43. For a more acceptable approach see the references to Rahner and Laurentin in note 8 to chapter 7, above.

15. Cf. above, chapter 1, 12, and chapter 2, 29.

16. Cf. above, chapter 4, 64-8.

17. Cf. Donald L. Gelpi, *Pentecostal Piety,* New York: Paulist 1972, 91-3. On Ignatian discernment, see the references in note 38 to chapter 7, above.

18. Cf. above, chapter 1, 17 and chapter 3, 50.
19. John of the Cross, *Collected Works* (trs. K. Kavanaugh and O. Rodriguez), Washington D.C.: Institute of Carmelite Studies 1973, 723.